MURDER
ON MERSEYSIDE

For my distinguished friend and inspiration,
Mr Richard Whittington-Egan.

© Tom Slemen 2011
Published by The Bluecoat Press, Liverpool
Book design by March Design, Liverpool
Printed by Martins the Printers, Berwick

ISBN 9781908457004

ACKNOWLEDGEMENTS

The author would like to thank Kevin Roach of the
Liverpool Records Office for his assistance in the
researching of this book.

Tom Slemen

MURDER
ON MERSEYSIDE

THE BLUECOAT PRESS

CONTENTS

INTRODUCTION

Like every other English county, Merseyside has had its fair share of murders over the years. This casebook contains various accounts of individuals who broke the sixth Mosaic commandment – 'Thou shalt not kill' – and it also contains cases where it is difficult to establish if an act of murder was actually committed at all. Take the intriguing case of the Man in the Iron Tube, which refers to a Victorian corpse found in a sealed metal cylinder. How the nineteenth-century man came to be a canned corpse is still a mystery, as is the cause of his death. The murders detailed in this book span 168 years, from John Bellingham's vengeance-filled assassination of the Prime Minister in 1812, to the world-shaking assassination of John Lennon, which occurred in 1980.

It is sad to relate how violent crime on Merseyside and in the rest of the world has evolved since the days of Bellingham's crime, when Britain did not have a police force at all. In January 1992 Merseyside Police introduced Armed Response Vehicles (known as ARVs) into the region to tackle the alarming number of hold-ups and other firearms-related crimes, which seem to be proliferating in the cities of Britain. Nineteen national forces now use ARVs, which are armed with Heckler Koch carbines, the weapons the SAS used to storm the Iranian Embassy in London in 1980. The German-made firearm is highly accurate, self-loading, and fires 9mm handgun bullets. It is also equipped with a powerful Mag Lite torch for illuminating night-time targets. The Smith & Wesson Model 10.38 calibre revolver is also carried in the ARVs, and many other guns are becoming available to specialist police officers. In an interview with the *Liverpool Echo* in April 1994, Merseyside's then chief constable James Sharples gave a chilling warning to armed thugs: 'If you live by the gun, be prepared to die by the gun ... if there's a threat to the police or public we will shoot.'

In the year Mr Sharples made his remark, Merseyside Police had made a record number of gun seizures, which included a cache of automatic weapons found in a flat in the Fazakerley district, 80 Italian shotguns found in a Bootle house, four machine guns buried in Formby and 13 machine guns discovered at a flat in Everton. Since the 1990s, gun crime has sadly become more common throughout Britain, and on Merseyside this fact was brought home when 11-year-old Liverpool Rhys Jones was shot in the back by a teenager on 22 August 2007. Rhys had been on his way home from football practice with a few friends, and as he was crossing a pub car park in the Croxteth district of Liverpool, an 18-year-old on a bike held a gun at arm's length and fired three shots. One of the bullets struck young Rhys in the back, slightly above the left shoulder blade, and exited from the front right of his neck. Rhys's mother rushed to the scene of the shooting when she heard what had happened, but when she reached her son, he was already unconscious, and despite the repeated attempts of paramedics to resuscitate him, Rhys died 90 minutes later at Alder Hey Children's Hospital.

Sean Mercer, aged 18, was found guilty of Rhys's murder and sentenced to life imprisonment with a recommended minimum term of 22 years.

Today, in the twenty-first century, Merseyside Police oversee a county with an area of 647 square kilometres and a population of 1.4 million. The force has about 4,400 police officers, some 2,200 staff, 440 police community support officers and around 420 special constables. The force came into being in 1974 when the county of Merseyside was created, and at one time, in 2006, the Home Secretary suggested that Merseyside Police should merge with the Cheshire Constabulary, but this proposal was vehemently rejected.

One of the most interesting developments in Merseyside Police in the twenty-first century is the formation of the Matrix Disruption team. These are a crack unit of inspectors, sergeants and constables who are speedily dispatched to deal with the increasing incidences of gun crime, cash-in-transit robberies, large-scale drug operations and major crowd disorder, among many other situations. The force also deploys the famous police helicopter, which is, at the time of writing, a Eurocopter EC 135 helicopter, based at RAF Woodvale, Formby. The chopper forms the backbone of the Air Support Group, first set up in late 1989 to monitor the increasing incidence of high-speed vehicle pursuits. In recent years, there has also been talk of using unmanned miniature drone helicopters fitted with the latest imaging devices to monitor urban criminal gangs and various illegal activities on Merseyside.

Crime never sleeps, and the fight against it must go on. Merseyside Police, like every other force in the world, has to uphold the law, despite government cuts and the increasing sophistication of some very computer-savvy criminals who now use identity fraud, 'phishing' and computer hacking instead of jemmies and sawn-off shotguns to obtain their ill-gotten gains. Despite the technological age in which we are now living, the inner nature of most men and women remains in the Stone Age, hence we have air rage and road rage, and the stresses of modern life, and relationships, can still lead to a crescendo of domestic violence, sometimes with fatal consequences. Likewise, crimes of passion will always be with us, as well as cold-blooded murder. It's a sad fact that almost every day in the *Liverpool Echo*, the city's major newspaper, are shocking headlines about shootings and stabbings, too often reported in an almost blasé manner, because we have become so desensitised to the horror of these all-too-regular crimes.

When Beatrice Alice Rimmer was brutally murdered in her Wavertree home in 1951 (and there is a chapter detailing her murder in this book), the people of Liverpool and beyond were appalled and shocked by the crime, but today, such murders are so routinely reported in the media, we just turn the page or change channels.

Tom Slemen
Liverpool, 2011

THE RAINHILL PSYCHOPATH

What is a psychopath? According to the accepted textbook definition, it is a person who behaves violently or antisocially and shows no guilt or feelings for others. This does not mean that the psychopath exhibits these traits all the time; otherwise he or she would be easily recognisable as such. From the data we have on psychopaths, it is evident that the majority lead largely ordinary lives until some mental disturbance triggers a drastic personality change.

Another question: is there a dormant psychopath in all of us? Many familiar idiomatic phrases in the English language seem to indicate that we acknowledge a dark and dangerous force deep in the human mind that surfaces and takes control of the ego. We have all heard or used phrases such as, 'I don't know what came over me'; 'I must have been out of my mind'; 'I must have been mad'; or, 'He can't have been himself when he did that'. Another expression along these lines is 'I don't know what possessed me' – a throwback to medieval times, when possession by demons was sometimes cited as the cause of a bad deed. Of course, since the work of Freud and other psychiatrists, demonic possession has largely been explained away as a mundane personality disorder, but even with all the latest technological marvels at the psychoanalyst's disposal, the mechanisms of the mind are still shrouded in mystery.

So the honest answer to the original question concerning the nature of the psychopath is that nobody knows, and, very often, nobody knows until it is too late. Take the case of Frederick Bailey Deeming, a seemingly normal, good-looking young man with captivating blue eyes, wavy sandy hair, who loved to shower the opposite sex with gifts. But behind the charming persona there lurked a callous killer.

Frederick Deeming was born in Birkenhead in 1853, the youngest of a poverty-stricken family of seven children. In his teens he abandoned his home for a life at sea, working as a ship's steward. He travelled the world, and for some reason began to adopt several aliases such as Lawson, Duncan, Druin and Williams, to name but a few. On his voyages around the globe he was alleged to have stopped off in various countries to perpetrate a series of murders and frauds. On several occasions he was rumoured to have entered into marriage for financial gain, and always ended up killing his spouse before making off with the proceeds. There were also claims that Deeming once knifed a Zulu to death over some dispute in the South African Cape. On another occasion, he was said to have shot thirteen lions in a single day to satisfy the incredible bloodlust he was developing.

When the black-hearted seafarer gave up his occupation and returned home, he obtained employment as a plumber and gas-fitter and also found himself a pretty young girl called Marie James, who instantly fell for his good looks and married him. Though Marie bore him four children, Deeming later callously abandoned her and his offspring, and went across the Mersey to seek a new life and a new love.

In July 1891 Deeming took out a lease on a cottage called Dinham Villa at Rainhill, near St Helens, where he posed as an army inspector named Albert Williams who was supposedly acting on behalf of a Colonel Brooks. It wasn't long before Emily Mather, the landlady's 25-year-old daughter, took an admiring interest in dashing Deeming, and suddenly romance was in the air yet again. Pretty young Emily was enthralled by Deeming's tales of his seafaring days. At last she had met her ideal man ...

However, one day Deeming's abandoned wife and family turned up unannounced at the villa. With amazing calm, Deeming casually passed off Marie as his sister. Infatuated Emily swallowed the tale, and Deeming realised that drastic action was now needed to give some credibility to his story. Somehow Marie and the children had to be disposed of and he quickly hatched a plan. First he went out to buy a pickaxe and several bags of cement, then prepared himself to wait for the right moment. This came soon enough.

During the night, when his wife and four children were sleeping peacefully in their beds Deeming set to work. In his nightshirt he crept into their bedrooms and systematically began slitting their throats, though inexplicably he chose to strangle one of his daughters instead.

The next grisly task he performed was the entombment of the bodies. He hid the five corpses in the shallow graves he had created under the hearthstones of the kitchen floor, and later employed labourers to assist him in cementing over the kitchen's uneven flags. Deeming carried this off by explaining that Colonel Brooks hated uneven floors. Unknowingly, then, the labourers helped to entomb the only obstacles that had stood in the way of Deeming's romance with Miss Mather. When the newly surfaced kitchen floor had finally dried out, Deeming threw a party to which he invited his sweetheart Emily and several other guests. During the merrymaking, Deeming danced with the unsuspecting guests upon the graves of his wife and children. Later that evening he proposed to Emily Mather, who, with a slight blush, accepted and the couple were married at St Anne's Church, Rainhill, on 22 September 1891.

Shortly after the marriage Deeming became uneasy about living at Dinham Villa, fearing that his slowly decomposing victims might start to smell. He told Emily that he needed to vacate the house because 'the Colonel' had decided to occupy it after all. Having left Dinham Villa, Deeming for a short while moved into his new wife's home half a mile away. But it was not long before he started to get itchy feet again and he told Emily, that as an inspector of regiments, he had received correspondence from the British Army requesting him to be stationed in Windsor, Australia.

On 15 December Deeming and his wife arrived in Melbourne and travelled out to the city's surburban district of Windsor, where they found suitable accommodation in a rented cottage at 57 Andrew Street. The couple unpacked their bags, with Emily feeling quite content about her new life Down Under. Already, however, Deeming was plotting the next move in his infamous career. Nine days later, on Christmas Eve, he took an axe and brought it down six times on Emily's head. Then, to make sure she was finished, he cut her throat. Up came the hearthstone which was to become Emily's unmarked headstone.

Early in the following year Deeming packed his bags again and boarded a Sydney-bound steamer. On board ship he met beautiful young Kate Rounsefell, and before the steamer had reached Sydney Harbour, Deeming had won her heart. He proposed, offering her an impressive diamond ring. Kate, complaining of an excess of haste, turned him down; nevertheless she decided she wanted to get to know him better. Deeming told her he was going to join the goldrush in Western Australia, and that he would soon be a very wealthy man. Still, Kate was not sure about marriage, but promised she would follow him.

Meanwhile, back in Melbourne, a woman was enquiring about the vacant house at 57 Andrew Street. The landlord of the premises accompanied her to the address and allowed her to inspect the place. In the bedroom the landlord and the prospective tenant encountered the terrible stench of Emily's rotting corpse. The unscrupulous landlord claimed the smell was merely from dead mice, but the woman quickly left, feeling nauseous. With the help of another man, the landlord lifted up the hearthstone in the bedroom, and immediately the aroma of decaying tissue became much stronger.

The police were informed, and when they later broke up a layer of cement under the bedroom floor, they discovered a hollowed-out grave containing the doubled-up body of a woman. Police inquiries determined that the name of the house of horror's last tenant was a 'Mr Druin', who had mysteriously left without giving any notice. During a thorough search of the house, the police found a luggage ticket which they traced to a shipping clerk. He recalled booking a sea passage for a man who called himself 'Baron Swanston'.

The police in Melbourne lost no time in cabling the information to their colleagues in Perth. There, Detective George Gurney made further enquiries, and discovered that a 'Baron Swanston' had stayed at the city's Shamrock Hotel and furthermore had left a forwarding address – a house at Southern Cross in the Western Australian outback. Detective Gurney quickly telegraphed the police outpost at Southern Cross, and the following morning, two armed police constables rode to Fraser's Gold Mine and arrested Deeming. He reacted with outraged innocence, protesting, 'This is all a mistake!'

Deeming was bundled into a mail coach and the 200 mile journey to Perth commenced. During the journey to justice, news broke of the discovery of Deeming's butchered family at Dinham Villa in Rainhill, England. Shortly afterwards, Kate Rounsefell, who was on her way to meet her fiance, received a telegram from her sister warning her to go no further. Kate almost fainted when she realised how close she had come to a horrible death.

While awaiting trial Deeming spent most of his time making morbid sketches of gallows and reading from the Bible. Then a rumour circulated the prison alleging that Deeming had confessed to being Jack the Ripper. Despite the fact that Deeming was not even in London at the time of the Whitechapel murders, the newspapers had a field day, and the *Melbourne Evening Standard* soon ran the sensational headline: JACK THE RIPPER: DEEMING AT ALDGATE ON THE NIGHT OF THE WHITECHAPEL MURDERS.

The murder trial opened on 8 May 1892 at Melbourne Criminal Court. Deeming, referred to in court as Albert O Williams, was tried for killing his wife Emily, but he had not been charged with the Rainhill murders. His defence counsel, a young barrister named Alfred Deakin, later became Australia's Prime Minister three times. Deakin argued that Deeming was insane, and so could not be held responsible for his actions. But the rhetoric was useless. On the final day of the trial Deeming obtained the court's permission to address the jury, and for a whole hour, he maintained that he had not been given a fair trial, as the newspapers had already made up people's minds for them.

After 30 minutes of deliberation, the jury returned a guilty verdict.

On the sunny morning of 23 May 1892, Frederick Deeming walked to the scaffold smoking a large cigar, given to him by the hangman. By now his hair had turned white. By a dark coincidence, the name of the gaol where Deeming was to be despatched was Swanston — as in one of his aliases. Outside the walls of the gaol, a crowd of 12,000 had gathered to be the first to hear the news of the execution.

Deeming was strapped up and his hands bound together. His face was covered with the white cap, and the hangman deftly secured the noose around his neck. Seconds before the lever was pulled, Deeming was heard to whisper, 'Lord receive my spirit'.

THE BODY IN THE SACK

At 6pm on the evening of 10 December 1913, a little shop at 86 Old Hall Street, Liverpool, was closing for the day, and the staff were getting prepared to make their journeys home. The sign above the shop read: J.C. BRADFIELD & CO.

Tarpaulin manufacturer John Copeland Bradfield owned the shop, but he wasn't a man who liked to be stuck behind a counter all day; so he let his spinster sister, Christina, take care of that side of the business, while he spent most of his time supervising the industrial processes at the factory he owned in Great Howard Street.

Christina Bradfield was a priggish, but rather attractive woman of 40 – although she looked much younger – and a very conscientious manageress. Her staff of three comprised Miss Margaret Venables, the 21-year-old typist and secretary; George Sumner, a 20-year-old assistant and packer, and Samuel Elltoft, the 18-year-old shop-boy. Samuel did a little bit of everything, including helping to organise the chaotic mounds of horse-cloths and rope that accumulated in the stores.

Shortly after 6.10pm Miss Venables put on her hat and coat and hurried out of the shop to catch her train home. Miss Bradfield was counting the day's takings, while George Sumner was sweeping the shop floor, all the while glancing furtively at his female boss. Whether he was lusting after her, or the takings, is hard to say. But as she counted the golden sovereigns and the silver florins and ordered them into neat columns, he moved in closer to her, still sweeping, still undecided as to what he wanted. Meanwhile, his 18-year-old workmate was

17

putting up the shutters outside. It is not known if he witnessed the vile act that took place that night.

Inside the shop, Sumner finally snapped. Without warning, he threw down his broom and began to rip the clothes off Miss Bradfield, and then proceeded to sexually assault her. She screamed, and Sumner responded by picking up a circular pin of hard wood which was used for splicing rope, and used it to beat her head repeatedly until she fell silent. Sumner stood over the battered, half-naked corpse, and suddenly realised the enormity of his crime. He now had to dispose of the evidence. He instructed Elltoft to help him haul the body into a sack, and probably either reminded the teenager that he could be charged with being an accessory after the fact, or simply promised that his assistance would be rewarded with a sum from the takings.

The two men doubled-up the blood-spattered corpse and secured its position with a rope, before easing it into a sack. Elltoft then sewed up the sack, and over an hour later, George Sumner decided it was time to shift the body off of the premises. He had a plan: to put the body on a cart and dump it in the Leeds and Liverpool canal, which was only about half a mile from the shop. As Sumner was thinking about the disposal plan, there was a loud noise outside. The two terrified young men stood stock still, gaping at one another. Then Elltoft gave a sigh of relief as he realised that the gale-force winds that were blowing that day must have blown a shutter off the shop window. He went outside to retrieve it, and encountered an angry young man who was examining a dented bowler hat. The man was Walter Eaves, a ship's steward on shore-leave who had recently disembarked the ivory-hulled *Empress of Britain* at the Pier Head and had been patiently walking up and down Old Hall Street waiting for his girl to turn up.

Elltoft ignored Eaves and heaved the shutter back on to the shop window.

'Hey! Just a minute! Your shutter's ruined my new hat,' complained Eaves, angrily pointing to the dent in his new bowler.

Elltoft scurried into the shop to tell Sumner what had happened and a few moments later Sumner appeared at the door with Elltoft and quickly expressed an apology before giving Eaves a florin as compensation. As Eaves walked away, Sumner bid him goodnight and closed the door. They thought they had successfully got rid of a potential witness, but Eaves continued to pace up and down the street, waiting for his date to arrive.

Shortly afterwards Eaves heard a trundling noise, and glanced around to see Elltoft pushing a handcart up the street, followed by Sumner. As it passed under the yellowish gaslight of a street-lamp Eaves noticed the cart was supporting a suspicious-looking sack. The young steward watched as the vehicle turned right at the top of the road and disappeared into Leeds Street. He considered the possibility of a body being in the sack, but soon dismissed the gruesome thought from his imagination. He glanced at his watch yet again and resumed his pacing.

Elltoft pushed the cart down Pall Mall, which was deserted, and then past empty warehouses, where the gales from the Irish Sea whined and howled like a band of grieving banshees. The tumbling cart rolled on down the length of Love Lane and across a stretch of wasteland until it finally halted by the locks of the Leeds and Liverpool Canal. Here the murderer and his accomplice got hold of each end of the lumpy sack, and, after looking around once more to make sure there were no witnesses, tossed it into the freezing black waters of the canal. The shrieking winds made the splash inaudible.

Sumner and Elltoft then wheeled the cart back to the shop. That was that: by the next day, they believed, the corpse would be lost forever in the depths of the River Mersey — but they thought wrong. Despite all the measures that a killer can take to dispose of his victim, sometimes Murphy's Law (which states that if something can go wrong, it will) rears its head. On such occasions Launcelot Gobbo's remark in *The Merchant of Venice*, that 'Truth will come to light; murder cannot be hid long', begins to ring true. And this was so in the case of the Body in the Sack.

As it turned out, the body did not drift out of the canal and into the sea as was intended, but was caught up in one of the canal's lock gates, where it was discovered the following day at noon by Francis Robinson, the master of a barge. He initially thought the obstruction in the mechanism of Number 3 lock was a sack of foodstuff from one of the nearby warehouses, but after pulling it free with a boat-hook, Robinson recoiled in horror when he noticed a black-stockinged leg dangling out of the bag.

Back at the shop in Old Hall Street, Miss Venables and Mr John Bradfield were becoming more and more concerned about the missing manageress. George Sumner and Samuel Elltoft made the occasional amateurish attempt at feigning concern, too, before lapsing back into their calm and collected moods. Later that day, the police informed Bradfield of the macabre find, and shortly afterwards he identified his sister's body at the Prince's Dock mortuary.

It didn't take the police long to start putting two and two together, and in the early hours of the following morning they called at Elltoft's house in Windermere Street, Anfield, and arrested him. They also went to Sumner's residence in Boundary Lane off West Derby Road, but the murderer had already done a moonlight flit.

A manhunt was launched and every available policeman combed the streets of Liverpool for Sumner. Every dockland warehouse was thoroughly searched, as was every public house and boarding house. The fugitive's face was projected on to the screens of every cinema in the city, and a £50 reward was offered for information leading to his capture. An irresponsible rumour-monger claimed the wanted man was a stowaway on the New York-bound *Majestic*, and so the police boarded the ship and checked out all the passengers and crew. By a freak of coincidence, the ship's steward shared the same name as George Sumner, but it was quickly established that he was not the one the police were looking for.

Back in Liverpool the police discovered that the murderer had been using an alias and that his real surname was Ball. This new piece of evidence did not make the search any more successful, however and it seemed as if Miss Bradfield's assassin had vanished off the face of the earth. But events suddenly took a positive turn on 20 December, when George Ball was finally spotted – not by a policeman but by an old schoolfriend. Ball had shaved his eyebrows, and was wearing an eye-patch and cheap spectacles at the time, but still his old friend recognised him, and followed the killer into the Mersey Lodging House Company's establishment at 84 St James's Street. The police were informed of Ball's whereabouts, and they arrested him shortly before midnight.

The murder trial opened at St George's Hall on 2 February 1914. The defence Ball offered was a ludicrous yarn about a stranger who appeared in the shop and held him at gunpoint before clubbing Miss Bradfield to death and running off with the takings. Faced with the grim fact of having a bludgeoned corpse on their hands, the two men had no alternative but to throw the body in the canal, as they felt no one would believe their story.

Then Elltoft went into the witness-box and gave a different fictional account of that night's events, quickly followed by the damning testimony of Walter Eaves, the steward who had been pacing Old Hall Street on the night of the murder and who had witnessed the two men carting away the sack that had aroused his curiosity.

At the end of the trial, the jury brought in a verdict of guilty and Ball was sentenced to death. Elltoft, who was found guilty of being an accessory after the fact, was given an unprecedentedly lenient sentence, considering the hideous nature of the crime. He was sentenced to four years' penal servitude.

Until You Are Dead

On the evening of 11 August 1873 a 29-year-old Liverpool boxer by the name of James O'Connor left Cambridge Music Hall at Mill Street in the south end of the city. The concert had ended and as the audience spilled out on to the streets, O'Connor noticed an attractive woman emerging from the hall. On an impulse, he asked her to accompany him to a public house to have a drink and an intimate chat. The woman, Mary Fortune, was married and, politely rejecting O'Connor's advances, walked on into the night. O'Connor could not take no for an answer and followed her down the street. He suddenly confronted the woman, accusing her of having had some money from him. Embarrassed, the woman turned around and started arguing with O'Connor, whereupon he suddenly struck her in the face twice; the force of the second blow knocking her to the ground. Two passers-by on the opposite pavement witnessed the assault, and one of them, James Gaffney, ran across the road and asked O'Connor why he had hit the woman. O'Connor made no reply, and instead reached into the inside pocket of his jacket and produced a clasp knife. Before Gaffney could raise his arm to defend himself, O'Connor had thrust the knife into his neck. Gaffney's friend, a man by the name of Metcalf, also ran over the road and tackled O'Connor. Metcalf delivered a straight punch to O'Connor's jaw that sent the boxer to the floor; however, being well versed in the art of pugilism, O'Connor was quick to recover from the blow, got back to his feet and plunged the knife into Metcalf's torso.

Gaffney and Metcalf were taken to the Southern

Hospital. Metcalf recovered, but Gaffney's internal bleeding could not be stopped, and he died the following morning.

After taking statements from Metcalf and Mary Fortune, the police were swift in tracking down O'Connor, who was a well-known trouble-maker with a fondness for blades. He was arrested and charged with Gaffney's murder and the attempted murder of his friend Metcalf. Before Judge Brett at the Assizes at St George's Hall, O'Connor was found guilty of both charges. He was sentenced to hang at Kirkdale Gaol early in September. O'Connor resigned himself to his fate, but he could not have imagined the mental torture that he would have to endure before his demise.

At 8am on the Monday morning of the execution the public executioner, an experienced man by the name of Calcraft, who had hanged thousands in his career and supervised several mass-hangings at Tyburn, took O'Connor and a priest on to the scaffold in the corner of the prison yard and led the condemned man on to the trapdoors. O'Connor stood there smiling and shivering in the freezing morning air before six pressmen as the priest, Father Bronte, prayed. Before the white cap was put on O'Connor's head, Father Bronte offered him a crucifix to kiss, which O'Connor did with apparent devotion. Calcraft then placed the noose around O'Connor's neck and drew it tight, then bound his wrists and legs with thick leather straps.

Father Bronte had just started reciting another prayer, when there was a crash, as Calcraft drew the bolt. O'Connor fell to what should have been certain death – but the rope snapped. O'Connor wriggled about in the pit below the scaffold, screaming in pain. Being bound, and blinded by the hood, he was confused to say the least, and for a moment thought he had passed over to the other side. Father Bronte jumped down into the pit with one of the reporters. The cleric pulled back the hood from O'Connor's head and tried to console him as he loosened the noose from his rope-burned neck.

O'Connor ignored the priest and turned to the pressman with tears in his eyes, saying, 'I stood it bravely didn't I? You'll let me go off now, won't you?'

The priest bowed his head and almost broke down as he patted O'Connor on the shoulder.

The journalist gave no answer, but scribbled O'Connor's desperate words in his notebook.

'What do you call this?' screamed O'Connor hysterically, when it began to dawn on him that he would not be let off. 'Do you call this murder?' he went on, and broke down, sobbing.

As Calcraft went to fetch another rope, Father Bronte tried to draw O'Connor's attention to an extract from the Book of Devotions, but O'Connor started ranting, 'I have not got over the pain! Lord have mercy upon me!'

The pressman jotted a few more notes and left the pit knowing that the half-hanged man was doomed to suffer the agonies of a second drop, because the law was specific and absolute on the matter: 'There to be hanged by the neck *until you are dead*.' And the law was to be obeyed.

Within minutes, James O'Connor found himself standing on the trapdoors once more with a noose of new rope about his neck, and the second time around the condemned had adopted such a defeatist attitude that Calcraft allowed him to adjust the noose himself and pull the white cap over his face. Seconds before the bolt was drawn, he stood there with his head bowed. When he fell for the second time, O'Connor took eight minutes to die, because Calcraft had made a gross error in calculating the length of the rope. He had only allowed for a drop of eight inches. Because of this second serious blunder, the hangman was never asked to despatch anyone again at Kirkdale Gaol.

WHO KILLED JULIA WALLACE?

William Herbert Wallace was born to lower-middle-class parents at Millom in Cumbria on 29 August 1878. His first job was as a draper's assistant in Barrow, but having an ambitious mind, he found the occupation boring, and longed for grander things in life than a future in the fabrics industry. He dreamt of an exciting and more fulfilling life abroad, such as the one his younger brother Joseph led in Shanghai, working as a printer for the British Government.

By the autumn of 1903, 25-year-old William Wallace left England's shores for Calcutta, where he had landed a job at the outfitters Whiteway and Laidlaw. This career move was a disaster. The climate was unbearably hot and the hours were long with low pay and virtually no prospect for promotion. Wallace's troublesome left kidney was also bothering him again. He decided to put in for a transfer to the Shanghai branch of Whiteway and Laidlaw, and his application was accepted, but agonising pains in his faulty kidney caused him nothing but grief, and he was advised by doctors to return to England for renal treatment. In the winter of 1907, he resigned from the overseas outfitters and sailed home. Within weeks of his return, he was sent by his doctor to Guy's Hospital in London to have his left kidney removed.

Wallace was an avid reader of the classics, and one of his favourite books was the *Meditations*, written by the ancient Stoic philosopher Marcus Aurelius. Wallace strongly identified with Stoicism, which advocates freedom from passion and desire, and he adopted the

Stoic creed, which is: Don't expect too much out of life, but strive to improve it by discipline and hard work.

Wallace later became a Liberal Party election agent in Yorkshire, where he met a pretty dark-haired woman named Julia Dennis. On 24 March 1914, after a courtship lasting three years, 36-year-old William Herbert Wallace married Julia. He seems to have been under the impression that she was just a year older than himself, but she was not 37 at all; she was, in fact, 52 years of age. She had lied about her age. The age difference was probably of no consequence anyway to two people in love, but William would have been unaware that his new wife was almost definitely beyond child-bearing age. On 28 April each year, William would celebrate his wife's birthday, unaware that he was marking a birth date that was almost 16 years behind the real one.

The outbreak of the First World War put paid to Wallace's job as an agent for the Liberal Party, as politics took a backseat to one of the greatest conflicts in the history of the planet. William Wallace never saw active duty in the war, possibly because of the precarious state of his health after the removal of his kidney; he continued to have problems with the remaining kidney until it would one day fail, with fatal consequences, when he was in his early fifties.

Less than a year after the wedding, Mr and Mrs Wallace moved to Liverpool, where William had, through the influence of his father, landed a job with the Prudential Assurance Company as an insurance collection agent for the Clubmoor area of the city. Before retirement, William's father Benjamin had himself worked for the Prudential, or 'the Pru' as it was nicknamed in those times. The Wallaces lived at 26

Pennsylvania Road in the Clubmoor district, but moved out after just four months to live in a red-brick terraced house at 29 Wolverton Street, a rather dreary-looking cul-de-sac in the Anfield area.

The couple rent the house for fourteen shillings and three pence per week, and from this period onwards, William Herbert Wallace lives in a clockwork world; settling into routines ruled by the clock. He dabbles in chemistry, and has converted a back room in his house into a small laboratory. He also plays the violin as a hobby, but isn't very good at it. Julia plays the piano in the parlour, and without a doubt she is the better musician. This musical leisure time in the parlour is allotted a set amount of minutes rather than hours. For 16 years, Wallace held the same job without promotion, and throughout this period the couple led a contented, but rather humdrum life of routines that were governed by the clock; breakfast time, lunchtime, worktime (for Wallace, but Julia stayed at home), leisure time, teatime, suppertime, bedtime. Almost every week, William would play chess at the Liverpool Central Chess Club, which met at Cottles Cafe, 24B North John Street, in the city centre.

On the wintry Monday night of 19 January 1931, William Wallace left his terraced Anfield home and rode a tram to the city centre, where he was due to play a game of chess at Cottles Cafe. At home, his wife Julia was recovering from a bad cold. At 7.15pm that Monday evening, a man entered a telephone box on Breck Road, just 400 yards from Wolverton Street. He lifted the receiver and asked the operator to connect him to Bank 3581, the number of the cafe where Wallace was to play chess. There was a technical hitch, so the operator recorded the number of the caller's telephone box: Anfield 1627.

At 7.20pm, the phone rang at the chess club and waitress Gladys Harley answered. A man's voice asked: 'Is that the Central Chess Club?'

Miss Harley said it was. The caller asked for a 'Mr Wallace', and Harley beckoned the club captain Samuel Beattie to come to the phone. Beattie, a cotton broker's manager, had known Wallace for eight years, and suspected that the caller wanted to discuss insurance business with his friend.

Beattie cleared his throat with a cough and spoke into the receiver: 'Samuel Beattie, club captain here. May I help you?'

'Is Mr Wallace there?' the caller enquired.

Beattie said he wasn't, then suggested the caller should ring up later when Wallace was due in.

'Oh no, I can't. I'm too busy,' said the caller, 'I have my girl's twenty-first birthday on, and I want to do something for her in the way of his business. I want to see him particularly. Will you ask him to call round to my place tomorrow at seven-thirty?'

Beattie asked the caller for his name and address. The answer he received was: 'The name's Qualtrough, R M Qualtrough.' And the address given was 25 Menlove Gardens East, Mossley Hill.

At 7.45pm, William Wallace came into the chess club and Beattie passed on the message from Qualtrough, a man whom Wallace professed never to have heard of, but the prospect of earning a 20 per cent commission on an annuity for his daughter was soon looking irresistible to Wallace.

On the following evening at 6.45pm, Wallace took

two tram journeys to Menlove Avenue. He could find a Menlove Gardens North, South and West, but no Menlove Gardens East. He made several enquiries in Mossley Hill, but the locals told him the address he was looking for did not exist – there was no Menlove Gardens East. Wallace returned to Wolverton Street, and found that the front and back doors of his home were locked against him.

He decided to try the back door once again. It took him 30 seconds to reach the back door from the front of his house. He met his neighbours, John and Florence Johnston as he came down the alleyway and told them how the doors of his home were locked against him. Mr Johnson asked Wallace if he had tried the back door. Wallace said he had but it had been locked. 'That's funny, try it again, and we'll wait,' said Johnston. 'If you can't manage to get it open, I'll see if my key fits.'

Wallace tried the back door again – and this time the handle turned and the door opened. The insurance collector rushed into the house. Not long afterwards he found his wife Julia lying dead in the front parlour. She had been horrifically bludgeoned to death.

Wallace called in the Johnstons, who would later tell the police that they had been leaving their backyard on their way to see their daughter in Townsend Avenue, West Derby, when Wallace had bumped into them.

'Oh, you poor darling,' Flo Johnston said, as she knelt beside her dead neighbour and felt her wrist for a pulse. John Johnston stood in the parlour doorway. 'Is she cold?' he asked. It seemed a somewhat insensitive question, but Florence nodded, upon which Mr Johnston said: 'Don't disturb anything, love. I'm going for the police.'

Mr Wallace asked his neighbour to call upon a doctor

as well. Mr Johnston said: 'Any particular doctor Mr Wallace?'

And Wallace grumpily replied, 'The nearest one!'

Johnston didn't go off immediately. He lingered around the kitchen, where the murderer had evidently wrenched off the door of a cabinet containing photographic equipment. The homicidal intruder had also rifled a small cash box that had usually contained the insurance man's takings. Four pounds had been stolen, and the burglar had taken the trouble to replace the cashbox on the top shelf. After Wallace had examined the box, Mr Johnston said: 'You'd better see if everything's all right upstairs before I go for the police.'

Wallace rushed upstairs, leaving the Johnstons in the kitchen. He returned a few minutes later and said that five pounds kept in a jar in the spare bedroom hadn't been stolen. Mr Johnston then asked: 'Was the light on in the [front] kitchen when you got back?'

'No,' Wallace replied, 'I put it on, and the one in the parlour.'

A few minutes later, Johnston called at Dr Dunlop's surgery on Lower Breck Road, but Dunlop told him this was a job for a police surgeon. Johnston therefore hurried on to Anfield Road bridewell, where he told a PC Saunders about the murder.

Back at the Wallace's kitchen, Mrs Johnston suggested brewing a pot of tea. Wallace just sobbed. 'Well, we'll have a fire!' Mrs Johnston shouted, and put woodchips and coal on the kitchen hob fire.

About ten minutes later, PC Fred Williams arrived at the house in Wolverton Street by bicycle. He began quizzing Wallace and the Johnstons, and shortly afterwards was joined by several detectives. Wallace told them how he had last seen his wife alive at a quarter to seven, but at 9.50pm, the insurance man's story was apparently blown apart by Professor MacFall. The police pathologist analysed the blood clots around Julia Wallace's head, then calmly announced that the woman had been dead since about six o'clock, perhaps before.

To the police, this damning estimation given by MacFall meant William Wallace couldn't have last seen Julia alive at a quarter to seven. Now let us go forward nine years in time for a moment.

On the night of 19 June 1940, a fierce aerial battle raged over East Anglia as a force of British aircraft met a fleet of Nazi bombers. The losses on both sides were severe. One casualty was a Blenheim night fighter, piloted by a 23-year-old Liverpool man, Sergeant Alan Croxton Close. The gunner parachuted to earth, but Sergeant Close bravely remained at the controls of his plane as it went down in flames. He aimed his injured craft away from the village at King's Lynn and saved many lives through sacrificing his own. It wasn't the first time Alan had saved someone's life. Nine years before, in 1931, Alan Close had saved the life of William Herbert Wallace.

On the night of his wife's murder, the case against William Wallace looked very bleak. He claimed he had last seen his wife alive at 6.45pm when he embarked on the fruitless journey to meet a client named Qualtrough in Mossley Hill. However, a bungling forensic 'expert' - Professor MacFall, a man who had a history of opium addiction, had calculated that Julia Wallace had been dead at 6pm, possibly before, which meant that Wallace was lying. Shortly after 10pm that traumatic evening, Detective Superintendent Hubert Moore – Head of CID –

turned up at Wallace's home in a drunken state. When MacFall told Moore how long Julia had been dead, the CID chief quizzed Wallace in the kitchen. In his mind, Moore believed Wallace was the killer. I have seen the official notes and marginalia that Moore made in his notebook, and without a doubt, he thought Wallace had murdered his wife and had tried to make it look as if a burglar had killed her. What Moore didn't know was that Professor MacFall had grossly miscalculated Julia Wallace's time of death. MacFall had not bothered to take the temperature of the body or the parlour. Instead he thought the blood clots around Julia Wallace's head 'looked quite old'.

Moore lifted the emptied cash box down from the top shelf in the kitchen and remarked, 'You know, I cannot for the life of me understand why a thief would go to all that trouble of putting the lid back on the box and placing it back where he'd found it.' When Moore later discovered that the call to Wallace's chess club had been made from a call box on Breck Road, he was ecstatic. It had to be Wallace. That phone box was a mere 400 yards from his home.

Wallace was subsequently arrested, charged with his wife's murder, and put on trial. His only hope of salvation came from the testimony of the 14-year-old milk boy – Alan Croxton Close. It transpired that he had delivered a can of milk to Julia Wallace on the night of her murder – at a quarter to seven. Julia had talked to Alan about his cough when he called. What's more, James Allison, a second youngster delivering the *Liverpool Echo* to the house next door to the Wallaces distinctly remembered Alan chatting to Mrs Wallace on her doorstep around 6.40pm.

When Detective Superintendent Moore heard about Alan Close's testimony, it cut him to the bone. All the same, Wallace was still arrested, and later put on trial for the murder of his wife. During the summing up by Justice Wright, one juror was sound asleep. The Judge tried to direct the jury to return a Not Guilty verdict. The jury retired, talked mostly about the perks they'd enjoyed as jury members, then returned with a verdict of Guilty. The court and Justice Wright were stunned by the verdict. The death sentence was read, and Wallace was whisked away to Walton Gaol in a Black Mariah.

The insurance agent lost no time in appealing against the sentence, and the unbelievable happened; the Court of Appeal quashed the conviction that had condemned Wallace, which was unprecedented. There is no doubt that the testimony of Alan Close was highly instrumental in saving Wallace from the hangman's noose. However, William Wallace's troubles were far from over.

In order to get to Menlove Gardens on the night of his wife's murder, William Wallace would have had to have left home no later than 6.49pm, yet milk boy Alan Close had spoken to Julia Wallace at 6.45pm, so if we are to believe that Mr Wallace killed his wife, he would literally have had about four minutes to bludgeon her to death – whilst wearing nothing but a mackintosh. We would then have to accept that Mr Wallace – who was a heavy smoker with only one kidney (which was afflicted with a chronic renal condition) could take a bath, get dressed, fake a break-in, dump the murder weapon (which was never found) bolt the front door, lock the back one, then sprint all the way to the tram stop.

This scenario, is of course, absurd, and the Court of Criminal Appeal thought so too, which is why Wallace's death sentence was quashed. Unfortunately, the people of Liverpool and beyond stuck to their firm belief that Wallace had killed his wife, and when the insurance agent was given back his old job at the Prudential, colleagues he had known for years treated him like a convicted criminal. Customers also refused to answer the door when he called, and people turned their backs on him in the street. They could not accept that Wallace was an innocent man who had found himself at the centre of a living nightmare.

If William Wallace didn't kill Julia, then who did? Thirty-two-year-old Ian Forbes of Crown Street, Edge Hill, gave himself up at Prescot Street police station on 14 May 1931 and admitted he had killed Julia Wallace. He was a methylated spirits drinker who was later found to be schizophrenic, and who had been nowhere near Anfield on the murder night. Then a James Gilmore, also aged 32, confessed to the murder. He was later admitted to Rainhill Mental Hospital. There were many more false confessions from an assortment of dreamers and cranks.

One such fantasist was Richard Gordon Parry, a 22-year-old amateur actor who had once worked for the Prudential insurance company with Mr Wallace. It has been alleged by countless authors and theorists that Parry was Qualtrough, and that he had sent Wallace on a wild goose chase just to get him out the house so he could kill Julia and frame her husband. In fact, Parry had not been in the Wallace's house for two years. A dubious rumour claimed that Parry had worn an oilskin coat, gauntlets and wellington boots as he clubbed Julia, but the forensic investigation established that there were no distinctive blood trails created by blood dripping off a waterproof surface on to the parlour carpet. Parry travelled in a car, yet no car was seen anywhere in the Wallace's neighbourhood on the night of the killing.

All the books and theories concerning the Julia Wallace murder do not reference the following curious fact. The police thought the circumstances surrounding the killing of Julia Wallace had an eerie parallel with a burglary that had taken place weeks before and just four doors away from the Wallace's home in December 1930. Samuel Shotton, a retired postman, had returned from holiday with his wife Clara to find their house at 19 Wolverton Street burgled, yet there had been no forced entry, even though the perpetrator of the crime had needlessly tossed pillows and blankets from the bed up in the Shottons' spare room – creating the impression that the burglar was a disorganised soul who had been rummaging about for money and valuables. The person who had burgled Samuel and Clara Shotton's home in Wolverton Street had known exactly where the couple kept their savings, and he had also known that the couple were away on holiday, almost as if he had inside knowledge, and what's more, he had even gone to the trouble of replacing the lid on the box that had contained the savings.

Now, up in the Wallaces' spare room on the night of the murder, the pillows and blankets were found in disarray, even though Julia Wallace's expensive mink coat and jewellery were found untouched in a drawer in that room. It seemed as if a duplicate key had been used to gain access to Wallace's home on this occasion as well. It is also worth noting that there had been a similar series of burglaries at the beginning of 1930 in Wolverton Street and some of the surrounding streets, and a 'skeleton key' was used in each robbery.

So who could have had such a duplicate key? John Sharpe Johnston, the next-door neighbour of William Wallace did and that is why he said: 'Try my key' when Wallace had bumped into him in the alleyway on the night of the murder. Wallace had told Mr Johnston that his back kitchen door had been locked when he tried it 30 seconds before, yet when he retried that door-handle – at the suggestion of Mr Johnston – he was baffled to find that someone had just unlocked it. I believe that person was John Sharpe Johnston. I believe he killed Julia Wallace, and being a next-door neighbour, 'Qualtrough' was able to leave the scene of the crime in seconds to walk eighteen feet down the backyard of the murder house into his own backyard. This would explain why Qualtrough went to ground so fast after killing Julia Wallace, and why he was never seen running or hurrying away from the scene of the crime by one single witness in the area.

With this hypothesis in mind, let us revisit the night of the murder. Wallace, upon his return from the fruitless quest for the fictitious Qualtrough at the non-existent Menlove Gardens East, goes to the front door of his home, only to find that it is locked. He goes to the back of the house via the alleyway to find the backyard door unbolted, which is odd, because Julia always bolts that door when her husband is out. Wallace walks up the yard, tries the back kitchen door; and finds it locked. He returns to the front door, which is still locked. He then takes just 30 seconds to walk to the back of the house to try his back kitchen door once again, and Mr and Mrs Johnston happen to emerge from their backyard door with perfect timing. John Sharpe Johnston has just unlocked the back kitchen door and walked just a few feet to his own backyard door where he and his wife wait to intercept Wallace. John Johnston had just washed and has changed his clothes. So has his wife Florence, for they both admitted to this at the ensuing court trial. Their excuse is that they washed and dressed because they were about to visit their daughter in West Derby – and were ready to embark on the tram journey at 8.45pm. However, Phyllis, their daughter, admitted she was not expecting her parents to call that night, and when they did call, it was usually between 6pm and 7pm. John Sharpe Johnston and his wife were not in the habit of calling upon their daughter or anyone else at such a late hour as almost 9pm, because Mr Johnston had to be up early to travel on an arduous route by tram and ferry boat to Cammell Laird shipyard on Wirral, and was often in bed by eleven at the latest and up at 4am.

The behaviour of the Johnstons on the night of the murder speaks volumes. Reading through the official files and the court transcripts of the Wallace case, the couple act somewhat out of character from the moment they meet William Wallace in the alleyway. Wallace tells them he can't get into his house, and enters his backyard to try the back kitchen door he had tried less than a minute ago, and John Johnston, standing in the doorway of the backyard with his wife, tells Wallace to *try the back kitchen door again*. 'Try it again and we'll wait here,' Mr Johnston says, 'If you can't manage to get it open I'll see if my key fits it.'

And, as if by magic, Wallace turns the handle of the back kitchen door and it opens effortlessly. John Johnston's suggestion to try his key to open the door of his neighbour's back kitchen leads us to one of those little-known facts surrounding this classic case which I have unearthed. In 1929, the Wallaces discovered, to their horror, that some of the keys to the houses in Wolverton Street fitted their own doors. On one occasion, a drunken neighbour, Mr Samuel Cadwallader, from 33 Wolverton Street, used his key to enter the Wallace's house one night as the couple were in bed. Julia screamed hysterically and the inebriated Mr Cadwallader apologised for his unintentional entrance into the house, which he mistakenly believed to be Number 33. Not long after this, Mr Cadwallader passed away, so we can discount him as a suspect, but he was a friend of John Sharpe Johnston, and it is reasonable to assume that Johnston would have been aware of the security vulnerability of the locks on the doors of Wolverton Street. Wallace mentioned this security issue to the police after the murder, and admitted that he had not bothered to have his locks changed after the incident, because he trusted his neighbours.

Wolverton Street residents Samuel and Clara Shotton, who had had their house burgled just before Christmas 1930, were also very trusting towards their neighbours – and had actually informed the Johnstons to keep an eye on their home while they were away. The police never regarded the Johnstons as suspects because the pathologist John Edward Whitley McFall had wrongly estimated the time of Julia Wallace's death, pointing the finger of suspicion at William Wallace. The insurance agent's version of events for the night of the brutal murder simply didn't add up if Julia was dead before he had left the house.

If the police had checked the Johnstons out they would have uncovered a couple of curious postcards in their sideboard, which came to light in the 1940s. These postcards are of interest because they completely contradict the testimony of the Johnstons when Edward Hemmerde KC, Counsel for the prosecution, asked the couple at the trial at St George's Hall, if they knew the Wallaces well. John Sharpe Johnston said he hadn't even known Mrs Wallace's first name was Julia, and Hemmerde then asked the Johnstons how many times they had been in the Wallaces' home during the ten years they had lived next door to them. Just three times, Florence Johnston had told Hemmerde. 'What? Just three times in ten years?' retorted an apparently surprised Hemmerde. Florence and John maintained that they had sat in the parlour of the Wallaces just three times in ten years, and, Florence was careful to add, they had not been in any other part of the house, such as the kitchen where the rifled cash box had been kept. The Johnstons created the impression that the Wallaces were virtually strangers to them. The Johnstons never explained two postcards sent to them by Julia Wallace while she holidayed with her husband in Anglesey, postmarked 23 July 1926 and 6 July 1928. The 1926 postcard, addressed to Mrs Johnston, reads: 'This is a lovely place, and we have such a nice place to stay ... best wishes to all' – and it is signed 'J. Wallace'.

The second postcard, sent to Mrs Johnston from Julia from Port Padrig, Cemaes Bay, Anglesey, in 1928, is more interesting. It contains an apology from Julia for not leaving Florence Johnston any money to buy food for Puss, the Wallaces' cat, and Julia promises she will pay her the money she owes her as soon as she returns from Anglesey. It turns out that the Johnstons were also entrusted with keys to open and close curtains at the Wallaces' home each day (to create the impression

41

someone was in the house and discourage burglars) and to collect mail during the fortnight's holiday. So it is not beyond the bounds of probability to suggest that the Johnstons mooched about in Number 29 Wolverton Street while the Wallaces were on holiday, and perhaps found the fabled nest egg that Wallace was said to keep somewhere in the house. Wallace was a known penny-pincher who lived on less than four pounds per moth, and his miserliness was something of a running joke to those few people who knew him. What was Wallace doing with the money he was saving?

Back to the night of the murder; when William Wallace entered his home via the back kitchen door, John Johnston and his wife Florence, stood in the backyard and after a minute or so they heard Mr Wallace calling his wife's name twice, then saw the light in the middle bedroom's upstairs window flare up. Then the Johnstons saw the light of a match being struck by Wallace in the window of the smaller upstairs room which the insurance agent used as a laboratory, and where he taught himself chemistry as a hobby.

Less than two minutes later, Wallace came out of the back kitchen into the backyard looking very distressed. 'Come and see!' he cried out. 'She has been killed!'

'What is it?' Johnston asked. 'Has she fallen downstairs?'

The Johnstons follow Mr Wallace into the house via the back kitchen, then into the front kitchen, out into the hallway, and into the front parlour, where the Johnstons see Julia Wallace on the rug with her brains pouring out, and Florence Johnston exclaims, 'Oh, you poor darling!' then feels for a pulse. Her husband John, standing in the parlour doorway, asks in a rather callous manner, 'Is she cold?' At this point, the killer could still be lurking in the dark house, but the Johnstons show no signs of being ill at ease. 'Would you like a cup of tea, Mr Wallace?' Florence asks, then makes a fire at the hob in the front kitchen as Wallace sobs. John Johnston surveys the aftermath of the burglary in the kitchen. Wallace shows him the cashbox and says he thinks four pounds has been taken, and then he points to a cabinet that had had its door wrenched off by the burglar. It had contained nothing but photographic equipment. Johnston then says to Mr Wallace: 'You'd better see if everything's all right upstairs before I go for the police and a doctor.'

But hadn't Mr Johnston already seen Wallace go upstairs when he stood in the backyard of Number 29 with his wife a few minutes ago? He had seen Wallace move with a lighted match from the middle bedroom window to the laboratory window. Given the horrific circumstances, an understandably confused Wallace obeys and goes upstairs anyway, leaving the Johnstons alone downstairs for a few minutes.

Mr Wallace then returns, saying, 'Everything's all right up there. There's five pounds in a jar they haven't taken.'

Johnston still lingers around the front kitchen for a while, then leaves his wife in the murder house as he goes, rather pointlessly, for a doctor (who tells Johnston to go straight to the police station on Anfield Road, as Mrs Wallace is obviously beyond medical help). The Johnstons had achieved their mission of getting back into the house to see if they had left any incriminating evidence from their botched burglary attempt. What was the evidence they had left? Well, police found a number of matchsticks next to the corpse and believed that, for some reason, the killer had struck a match to survey the fatal injuries he had inflicted upon his victim. The lingering killer had evidently dropped each match when it had burnt down and then struck another one. The first person to remark upon these matches was Florence Johnston, and she also asked Mr Wallace if the box of matches on the table by the parlour window were his or Mrs Wallace's – as the insurance man was still reeling in shock as he knelt by the body of his murdered wife. Wallace is so bewildered and disoriented by the nightmarish situation, he says the matches may be his, but he isn't sure. Why is Florence so fixated with such a trivial matter of matches when her next-door neighbour has just been bludgeoned to death and is lying on the floor with her brains oozing out of her smashed skull? Still, Florence persists, querying the ownership of the box of matches and asserting that they must belong to Mr Wallace. Are they in fact matches belonging to the Johnstons, left behind when they fled from the murder house? Are they the matches John or Florence struck after they came back into the house to see if Mrs Wallace was dead? Florence picks up the box of matches, planting her fingerprints on them before a witness.

In 1955, Fred Williams, the former policeman who had been the first to arrive at the scene of the murder at Wolverton Street, was being treated for influenza in Broadgreen Hospital when he recognised one of the consultants in the ward as Dr Robert Coope, a man who had investigated the crime scene of the Julia Wallace murder 24 years before. The retired policeman told Dr Coope he had something to tell him that had been playing on his mind for too many years. Williams was seriously ill, and had difficulty breathing, but managed to tell the doctor that he believed he knew who had killed Julia Wallace. He started by saying that Mr Wallace was innocent. Williams had only interviewed three people: Mr Wallace – and the Johnstons. Dr Coope was extremely busy that day and promised he'd come back to see the ex-policeman in the morning to hear his views on the old murder case, but Williams sadly died from influenza soon after making his intriguing comments, so we'll never know what he had to say.

The police could not work out why no blood splashes were found either outside the parlour in the hallway or on the living room door. It was as if some person had been standing between Julia Wallace and the door as she was battered to death. Could it be that Florence Johnston was standing between Julia and the doorway as her husband battered the woman's brains out?

In April 2001, I appeared on a programme on BBC Radio Merseyside about local crimes and appealed for people who had known the Johnstons to get in touch with me. A seriously ill man named Stan who had known John Johnston got in touch, together with local criminologist Keith Andrews. Stan said Johnston had died in January 1960 of senile dementia at an old people's home on Westminster Road. I have checked this information and found it to be true. Stan said that, days before Johnston died, he confessed to killing Julia Wallace. He admitted it was he who had made the Breck Road telephone call to the chess club to get Wallace out of the house. Florence had Julia's cat Puss and was supposed to lure Julia next door to get it. Julia's cat had been missing for days. But John Johnston had surmised that Julia had gone to Menlove Gardens with her husband when he saw them go out of the backyard together, because Julia had on a mackintosh. Julia had in fact been walking down the alleyway looking for Puss, and Johnston didn't see her return. The Johnstons waited for a while, then slipped into the Wallace's house via the back kitchen door, which John unlocked with his key. He went in search of the insurance man's monthly takings and a nest egg he believed to be upstairs. That nest egg, if it ever existed, was nowhere to be seen, and there were no monthly takings because Wallace had been off work with a bad cold and unable to collect the usual amount of money for that month.

Disappointed with the meagre haul, John and Florence decided to try the front parlour. As they entered they got the shock of their lives when the flu-stricken Julia Wallace rose from her couch with the mackintosh over her. She wasn't supposed to be there. 'Mr Johnston!' Julia probably shouted, alarmed and then puzzled as to why her neighbours were in her house. John decided to hit her with the jemmy he'd used to smash open the cabinet in the kitchen. He had to kill her, because she now knew the identity of the man who was burgling the neighbourhood. The only fingerprints that would be found at the murder scene belonged to Mr Wallace, the sloppy detectives and police – and the Johnstons.

On the following day, the Johnstons suddenly moved out of Wolverton Street and went to live with their daughter at 358 Townsend Avenue. Florence was subsequently treated for shingles and had treatment for what was then known as 'bad nerves'. Years afterwards, in the 1950s, the Johnstons moved to 13 Braybrooke Road, in West Derby. One day, a neighbour stopped at their garden gate to chat to Florence, and in the course of the conversation, the topic turned to the subject of the

Wallace murder. Florence Johnston said something about the world-famous case, and suddenly, her husband John Johnston, who had been standing in the hallway, obviously eavesdropping on the conversation of his talkative wife and the neighbour, came marching down the path. He dragged Florence into the house, and, according to the neighbour, when she next saw Florence, the woman sported two enormous black eyes. Not long after that, an ambulance called at the Johnstons. Florence was dead. According to Mr Johnston, his wife had awakened in the night complaining of pains in her upper arms. 'Go back to sleep, love,' Mr Johnston had told her, 'you'll be all right.'

The next day he found her dead in bed. She'd died from an embolism.

Raymond Chandler, the famous crime fiction writer, took a great interest in the Wallace case, and finding no solution, remarked that the murder could never be solved. I believe he was wrong. I believe that the one person who suspected the Johnstons of being Qualtrough was Edward Hemmerde KC, ironically the very man chosen to be Kings Counsel for the Prosecution. Hemmerde examined and re-examined the Johnstons, questioning them about the times they had visited the Wallace household: 'You say you knew the Wallaces as neighbours?'

'Yes,' Florence Johnston replied.

'Had you ever been in their house?' Hemmerde queried.

'Yes,' said a barely audible Florence Johnston.

'How often?'

'About three times.'

'In ten years you have been in *three* times?'

'Yes,' answered Florence Johnston, 'in the front room only, where the body lay; the sitting room.'

'Were they both there on those three occasions? The two of them?'

'No, only Mrs Wallace,' Mrs Johnston replied.

Hemmerde told the court that 'Qualtrough' had to be *two people*, as there was no single vantage point in the area of Wolverton Street where Qualtrough could position himself to positively ascertain whether or not William Wallace had left his home by the back or front door on the night he set out on what would turn out to be a hopeless quest for the non-existent address. Hemmerde suggested that if Qualtrough was, in fact, two people, one could watch the front of the Wallace house and the other could keep watch on the alleyway, and therefore be wholly sure that Mr Wallace had taken the bait and gone in search of the make-believe Menlove Gardens East.

Qualtrough was obviously acquainted with the layout of Menlove Gardens, enough to know that there was a Menlove Gardens North, a Menlove Gardens South, and a Menlove Gardens West, but no Menlove Gardens East. John Sharpe Johnston worked at the Cammell Laird ship-building yard in Birkenhead, and one of his close associates there was one Dan Roberts, a shipping clerk, who lived at 30 Menlove Gardens West. Mr Johnston had visited Roberts at his Mossley Hill home on many occasions – but those visits suddenly ceased after the murder of Julia Wallace.

The Johnstons were well acquainted with the domestic routines of the Wallaces. The partition wall separating their houses was so thin, the Johnstons admitted in court that they knew when Amy Wallace –

48

William's loud sister-in-law – was visiting, because they could hear her voice, and yet the Johnstons never heard the intruder smashing the cabinet in the Wallace's front kitchen, nor did they hear Julia being struck on the skull eleven times, nor the sound of her body falling to the floor. And nor did they hear anybody knock at the doors of the house – and yet, the Johnstons told the court that they clearly heard Wallace knocking on the front and back doors of his home when he couldn't gain entry on the night of the murder.

In 1931, Cammell Laird, John Johnston's employer, made only one vessel, as the knock-on effects of the Great Depression, which had started in the United States with the Wall Street Crash of 1929, reached Britain, with devastating results, especially for the northern industrial cities. The 1930s (up until the Second World War) saw the longest ever recession of the twentieth century. The outlook was bleak, money was hard to come by, and the crime rate soared as a result. I believe the murder of Julia Wallace was not a premeditated murder but the result of a robbery attempt that went horrifically wrong. I think the blunt weapon that killed Julia was the jemmy bar that John Sharpe Johnston used to wrench the door off the cabinet in the front kitchen, and when he found himself confronted with Mrs Wallace in the parlour, he probably lashed out as she tried to escape from him, as all of the eleven blows were concentrated on the back of her head, and the first one probably killed her. Had Mrs Wallace been allowed to live, she would almost certainly have reported her neighbour to the police, and Mr Johnston wouldn't have just been sentenced to gaol for a number of years, he would have lost any hope of future employment as well, and faced everlasting disgrace.

It would be terribly arrogant of me to claim that I had solved the Julia Wallace murder case. In all probability, we will never know the truth of the matter, but I do believe that John Sharpe Johnston should be seriously considered as a suspect in future studies of this classic cold case.

THE LEVESON STREET MASSACRE

One spring morning in the year 1849, 29-year-old music teacher Ann Hinrichson placed a notice in the front parlour window of her home at 20 Leveson Street. The notice read: 'Furnished Apartments to Let'.

Mrs Hinrichson's Danish mariner husband, John, was at sea on his ship *Duncan*, and so she was left with the formidable task of running the household and rearing her two sons, five-year-old Henry George and three-year-old John Alfred. What's more, Mrs Hinrichson was also expecting a third child. The fourth person living at the house was the maidservant Mary Parr, a conscientious and indispensable woman of 30, who helped to reduce Mrs Hinrichson's burden. As well as being a servant, Miss Parr was also a very trustworthy friend of Mrs Hinrichson.

Leveson Street, which ran from Great George Street to Suffolk Street, was a busy thoroughfare in the nineteenth century, and no doubt there were hundreds of passers-by who glanced at the card in the window at Number 20. But of all those individuals, only one called in to inspect the vacant rooms, and he was a 26-year-old Irishman from Limerick, who went under the name of John Gleeson Wilson.

Wilson was shown the front parlour and the back bedroom, and, finding them to his liking, he immediately paid a week's rent in advance and moved in. The Irishman claimed to be a carpenter employed by the Dock Estate, and Mrs Hinrichson was pleased at having such an upright and hard-working young man as a lodger. What Mrs Hinrichson didn't know was that

Wilson already had perfectly adequate lodgings in Porter Street, off Great Howard Street.

That night, at around ten o'clock, young Mr Wilson bade goodnight to Mrs Hinrichson and went to bed.

On the following morning Wilson rose early, and by 7.30am was in a nearby pub in Great George Street, having a glass of ale for his breakfast. At this public house, the first move that led to the wholesale slaughter of four innocent people and an unborn child took place. Wilson suddenly asked the pub's landlady if she could provide him with a wafer to seal an envelope containing an important letter.

'No, I'm sorry,' she said, 'but I've got a stick of sealing wax. Will that do?'

Wilson used the wax to fix down the flap of the envelope, then asked the landlady if she would be so kind as to write the address on the envelope, as he could not write. The proprietress was not exactly a skilled writer either, and called for her daughter. To the landlady's daughter, John Wilson dictated the address: John Wilson, Esq., 20 Leveson Street, Liverpool.

Shortly after leaving the pub, Wilson called to a passing youth named Edward McDermott and asked him if he wanted to earn a few pennies by delivering the letter. The teenager nodded enthusiastically, and in his charming Irish brogue, Wilson explained what he had to do. 'When I go into the house [in Leveson Street], I want you to wait a few minutes, then I want you to knock. Ask the person who comes to the door if John Wilson lives there, and say that you have a letter for him from his employer. Got that?'

The lad nodded. Five minutes after Wilson entered the house, the youth carried out his instructions. He approached the door of Number 20 and knocked. A few moments passed, then Miss Parr answered the door.

'Does John Wilson live here?' enquired the youth, as instructed by the deceptive lodger. 'Yes, here he is,' said Miss Parr. Wilson came to the door, and, after borrowing three pennies from Mrs Hinrichson to pay the errand boy, returned to his room with the letter.

At around 11am Mrs Hinrichson visited the shop of Mr Cox, her greengrocer, at 66 St James's Street and ordered some potatoes. Next, she called at Roebuck's the chandler's to purchase two jugs, which she asked to be delivered to her house. She then returned home.

Early that afternoon an errand boy named Anthony Carney arrived at Mrs Hinrichson's house with the potatoes. Wilson came to the door, took the vegetables off the boy, went into the house, threw the potatoes down on the parlour floor, then returned to the door with the empty basket.

Almost half an hour passed before Roebuck the chandler sent his son Daniel to Mrs Hinrichson's house with the purchased jugs. He rang the doorbell, but nobody answered. He lifted the knocker and brought it down hard several times over, but still nobody came to the door. The youngster then peeped through the keyhole — and saw a pair of feet lying across the hall. This made the him curious, so he climbed the railings in front of the parlour and looked in through the window. What he saw made his stomach turn. The parlour was like an abattoir. In scarlet pools lay the bodies of Mary Parr and little Henry. The errand boy almost fell from the railings with shock. He jumped down and ran off, looking for a policeman, and in Great George Street, the terror-stricken youngster ran straight into the arms of one.

'What's to do, lad?' said the policeman, trying to calm the terrified boy.

'Murder!' cried the boy, all out of breath.

'Eh? Now then, son. That isn't funny,' the policeman retorted angrily.

But the boy assured him that he wasn't making it up and urged him to come to the house in Leveson Street to see for himself.

Meanwhile a young girl who was a pupil of Mrs Hinrichson was arriving at the house for a music lesson. After getting no reply, she attracted the attention of a passer-by named John Hughes, a bricklayer by trade, who was visiting a relative on Leveson Street. The girl told him she thought something was wrong. Mr Hughes knocked several times, then looked through the parlour window. After seeing the same scenes of carnage that had sent the errand boy running for the police, Hughes broke a window-pane and made a forced entry into the house. Within minutes, other people from the street were swarming into Number 20, and when the policeman and the errand boy arrived at the scene, almost every inhabitant of Leveson Street was milling about near the house of horror.

Later that afternoon more policemen arrived to carry out a thorough search of the premises. The first body the police investigators encountered was that of Mrs Hinrichson. She was lying battered and stabbed in the hallway. In the parlour they found the maidservant, who was soaked in blood, having been battered about the head with a pair of coal tongs that were found lying nearby covered with clotted blood and strands of Mary Parr's hair. The maidservant was barely alive, but five year-old Henry, lying next to her, was not. He had sustained over 30 blows to his skull, and his head was greatly deformed by the savage attack, and his brains were visible. Furthermore, his little finger had been severed as he held his hands up in a defensive effort to protect himself from Gleeson's knife, and the tiny digit was found stuck to the little boy's clothes. Down in the cellar, the police discovered the tiny body of John Hinrichson. His throat had been cut from ear to ear, and his head was hanging by just a thread. Having witnessed the horrific death of his brother he had run downstairs in a futile attempt to hide from the killer in the cellar. The carving knife that had been used to almost decapitate the three-year-old was found lying next to his body. A bowl of scarlet-tinged water was found in Wilson's room with a poker lying nearby, coated in blood. The motive for the killings had undoubtedly been robbery, as it was later established that a large sum of money belonging to the absent John Hinrichson senior had gone missing.

Miss Parr was rushed to the Southern Hospital, where detectives waited for her to regain consciousness. She eventually came around, managed to recount what had taken place in the house that afternoon, then slipped into a coma.

It was recorded in the *Liverpool Mercury* and *Liverpool Albion* newspapers of 14 September 1849 that a strange incident had taken place in India on the day of the mass murder in Leveson Street. Captain John Hinrichson was enjoying a meal with several other merchant ship captains in Calcutta, when he suddenly stopped eating and pushed his plate aside. The captains saw that Hinrichson had a very concerned expression on his face, which suddenly turned pale. 'What is the matter?' one of them asked the Danish captain, and he said that by some feeling or impression he could not explain, he was convinced that something disastrous had just happened at his home.

Meanwhile, back in Liverpool, for some unfathomable reason, the killer went to Toxteth Park to wash his blood-spattered clothes and boots in the park's figure-of-eight pit, in full view of a number of witnesses. From the park he made his way to a shop on London Road where he sold a gold watch. With the money from the sale he bought himself a pair of trousers from a clothes dealer in Great Homer Street, then went to his lodgings in Porter Street, where he asked his landlady for a clean shirt. The landlady gave Wilson one of her husband's shirts, and became suspicious when she saw that her lodger's discarded shirt was stained with blood.

At six that evening, Mr Wilson called at a barber's shop around the corner in Great Howard Street for a shave, and while the barber was lathering his face, Wilson asked him if he had a wig to sell because his hair was coming out in tufts, and he tore bunches of his red hair out, then said to the barber, 'Do you see what I mean?'

The barber said he didn't sell men's wigs, but he knew of a shop in nearby Oil Street which supplied them and he told Wilson that he would take him there if he wished. On the way to the shop, which was only three streets away, Wilson said to the barber, 'Have you heard about the murder?'

'No, what murder?' replied the barber.

'A terrible affair,' said Wilson. 'Two women and two children had their heads bashed in.'

'How awful!' said the barber, disgusted. 'Did they get him?'

'No, not yet,' replied Wilson.

After purchasing a wig, Wilson took a ferry ride across the Mersey and went to Tranmere to spend the night with his estranged wife. The following morning, however, despite knowing that a police dragnet had been thrown over the city to snare the country's most-wanted and most-hated man, he again boarded a ferry and returned to Liverpool. Once across the river he visited the shop of Israel Samuel, a Great Howard Street watch dealer. Mr Samuel was an intuitive man, and felt rather uneasy about Mr Wilson, who wanted £6 for a gold watch. Mr Samuel called for a policeman and asked him to examine the watch. The policeman said the watch did not resemble any that had been reported stolen, but still Mr Samuel felt there was something about Mr Wilson that he couldn't put his finger on. He told Wilson that he had insufficient cash on the premises to pay for the watch. But before Wilson left, the watch dealer told him that if he went with his son to his other shop in Dale Street, he would be given the money there. Wilson nodded, and Mr Samuel took his son to one side and in Hebrew said, 'When you are passing the police station, collar this fellow and give him in charge.'

And so, as Mr Samuel's son walked past the police bridewell in Cheapside, off Dale Street, he grabbed Wilson and took him in. Wilson was totally taken by surprise.

At this time – 5 April 1849 – Miss Mary Parr, the Hinrichsons' maidservant died without regaining consciousness.

After a lengthy interrogation, Wilson was thrown in a cell. In the days leading up to his trial, he often flew into fits of rage, frothing at the mouth, and screaming that he was innocent.

Not long after this, Captain John Hinrichson arrived at St Helena in his ship *Duncan*, when a ship's purser approached him and said he had some very sad news for him. 'Well, these are my mates,' the master mariner replied, nodding to his crew members around him, 'I have no secrets, tell me the news before them.'

The messenger shook his head and beckoned the captain into his cabin. Hinrichson seemed bemused as he followed him into the cabin, where the brutal news was broken to him. 'Your wife, two children and maidservant have been murdered,' said the messenger.

At first the captain smiled, but then he suddenly fell down and pounded the floor with his fists. The *Duncan* took 59 days to reach Liverpool, and during that long voyage home, the captain hardly slept a wink. He would pace the deck, and was kept under constant supervision lest he try to take his own life. When the *Duncan* finally arrived at the Liverpool docks, the captain's closest friends and relatives were there to greet him. Captain Hinrichson wrung his hands and asked them, 'Where is my wife? Where is my Ann? Where is my little Harry and John Alfred?'

'Come home, John,' said Mrs Harrison, the mother of Ann Hinrichson.

'Home?' replied the heartbroken mariner. 'I have no home.'

After much persuasion from his friends and mother-in-law, the captain was taken to the house of a relative on Upper Pitt Street.

The murderer Wilson, meanwhile, was suffering from a severe cold and stiffness of the neck as he languished in his draughty cell at Kirkdale Gaol, awaiting trial. 'My neck is stiff, but I suppose they'll straighten it soon,' he joked. Two keepers, who stayed with him day and night in the cell, didn't even acknowledge the black-humoured remark. 'I wish the cholera would come and take me off with it!' Wilson cried.

A slow-witted janitor who had just come into the cell to fill his toilet bowl said, 'Oh, but it might take me off with it too.'

'Oh well, damn you,' Wilson told him. 'What loss would there be to the world if it did?'

Wilson was tried at Liverpool Assizes on 23 August 1849, before Mr Justice Patterson, and without leaving their box, the jury found him guilty of the four murders.

A letter arrived at the gaol shortly afterwards from the Sheriff, giving the date of Wilson's execution, and this information was communicated to the prisoner at once. 'Oh, damn them!' was Wilson's reply. 'Why do they not hang me at once? I'm tired of waiting!'

The Reverend Duggan of St Joseph's Catholic chapel, visited Wilson in his cell, and urged the prisoner to be repentant about his actions, but Wilson shouted back, 'I am not guilty!'

'Everybody believes that you are,' Father Duggan told him, 'and I also think so.'

'Damn you!' Wilson screamed at the priest, 'Get out of the place! I do not want you at all!'

Wilson told the two gaol keepers he was innocent of the four murders, but then he made a tell-tale remark which betrayed his false assertions. 'My mother was good, kind and so pious,' Wilson reflected with a tear in his eye. 'If she had lived, *none of this would have happened*. When she died, all went wrong.'

John Wilson, whose real name turned out to be Maurice Gleeson Wilson, was sentenced to hang on the Saturday morning of 15 September 1849. When that day came, a crowd of 50,000 people from all over the region gathered to see the execution of the most hated man in the country at Kirkdale Gaol. At around 11.30am the crowd fell silent as a white dove suddenly descended from the blue skies and landed on the crossbeam of the scaffold. The bird stayed there eyeing the mob for a while until it was startled by the approach of two men: the prison governor and a priest.

The governor had come into the prison yard to explain the working of the scaffold to the priest, who wanted to be assured that the condemned man would have a swift, humane death. Shortly before noon, Wilson was escorted by the under-sheriff from the condemned cell to the press room to meet the public executioner, a 70-year-old hangman from York by the name of George Howard. Howard was very incompetent and seemed more nervous than Wilson, fumbling with the straps as he bound the condemned prisoner.

The doomed convict was escorted to the scaffold outside by two priests, who recited the Litany for the Dying. Wilson's face was suddenly white as a sheet and he began to pray. The executioner followed closely behind, occasionally displaying a prominent nervous twitch in his face.

Wilson was positioned on the drop. Howard slipped the noose over his head wrongly, and had to adjust it so the knot was on the right side of Wilson's neck. Howard then pulled the white cap over his head, but it was too small, and only managed to cover the top of his head, just to his eyebrows. Howard then retreated to the release lever, trembling. The clergymen, who had been standing on each side of Wilson, began to recite their prayers in raised voices, and moved back, away from the condemned man.

Howard triggered the mechanism that drew the bolt back, and the Leveson Street murderer fell two feet as the trapdoor crashed away. A tremendous cheer went up from the crowd that faded as the spectators near to the execution witnessed Wilson's terrible death. Howard should have made the drop much longer than twenty-four inches. Wilson's death was slow and agonising because of the old executioner's incompetence. Wilson drew up his legs spasmodically, and because the white cap was not pulled over his face, some squeamish onlookers screamed and a few of them fainted as they saw Wilson's countenance become gruesomely distorted. His eyes bulged out of their sockets, and veins like purple knotted cords sprang up from his crimson cheeks. His blackened, elongated tongue hung out of his foaming mouth, and he emitted an awful choking sound. Howard suddenly reappeared and started pulling the white cap further down over the dying man's face, and Wilson's bulging eyes glanced sideways at the executioner in sheer horror, until they were finally covered. About 15 minutes later, the hanged man finally stopped moving.

Ann Hinrichson, her unborn child and her two sons were buried along with Mary Parr in the same grave in nearby St James's Cemetery.

Because of the notorious massacre associated with Leveson Street, crowds of morbid individuals made regular pilgrimages to see the house of blood at Number 20. To dissuade the ghoulish sightseers from visiting the infamous street, the council later renamed the thoroughfare Grenville Street. Today Grenville Street South is the only vestige of a street that was once synonymous with murder.

THE MAYBRICK TRAGEDY

She was a pretty young auburn-haired woman from Mobile, Alabama, and he was a wealthy middle-aged businessman from the respectable Liverpool suburb of Aigburth. She was 18-year-old Florence Chandler, and he was 42-year-old James Maybrick, and it was upon the luxurious White Star liner *Britannic,* in the year 1881, that their paths through life met.

The Liverpool-bound liner was ploughing across the icy expanses of the mid-Atlantic when James Maybrick first set eyes upon Miss Chandler, who was travelling alone. He approached her and introduced himself, and when she spoke, Mr Maybrick found her accent quaintly indeterminable. It seemed to contain elements of upper-class English and a hint of the Continental with an intonation redolent of the American South. Miss Chandler explained that her hybrid accent was the result of a cosmopolitan upbringing. During her formative years she had lived with various relatives in London, Paris and the other major European cities, as well as New York, where she had just been to see her grandmother. The faint Southern drawl was the legacy of a childhood spent in the sunny cotton fields of Alabama.

When Maybrick mentioned he was from Liverpool, Miss Chandler said she had been to the city to see the world-famous Grand National at Aintree, and she began to talk of horsemanship, which, by coincidence, was one of Mr Maybrick's main interests.

Seven days later, James Maybrick announced his engagement to Miss Chandler to the rest of the liner's passengers, and when the captain of the *Britannic* learned of the betrothal, he rang the ship's bell and proposed a toast to the couple's future.

Later that year, in July, the couple were married in London at St James's Church, Piccadilly, and they enjoyed a honeymoon in Brazil.

For several years the couple lived at Norfolk, Virginia, where Mr Maybrick conducted his business as a cotton-broker. Every morning he would leave Florence, who by now had a baby boy to look after, and head for his office at the Norfolk Cotton Exchange. But, unknown to his wife, James Maybrick did not always go directly to work. Most mornings he made little detours to various drug stores along Main Street to purchase arsenic, which he took regularly in small quantities, because he believed it fortified him.

On one occasion Maybrick was preparing a meal for himself when a friend saw him adding a grey powder to the food. When his friend asked him what the powder was, Maybrick casually replied, 'It is arsenic. We all take some poison more or less. For instance, I am now taking enough arsenic to kill you. I take this once in a while because I find it strengthens me.'

In 1884 the Maybricks returned to England and took up residence at Battlecrease House, in Aigburth's Riversdale Road. James Maybrick continued to prosper in his business, and he and Florence moved upwards into the exclusive circles of Liverpool's high society. They attended countless soirées, dances, dinner parties, horse races and numerous public events held at St George's Hall.

In 1886 Florence gave birth to a second child, a daughter named Gladys Evelyn, but the joy the new child brought was cut short when an epidemic of scarlatina hit Liverpool. Five-year-old James Maybrick, the elder child, was stricken with the fever. Because his father feared that his baby daughter would also contract the fever, he and a nursemaid took her to Wales, leaving Florence to tend little James. For six weeks Florence cared for her son and, in the end, thanks to her dedication, he pulled through.

But around this time, Florence was devastated to learn from one of the staff at Battlecrease House that her husband had a mistress somewhere in Liverpool and that, long before his marriage, this woman had given birth to two of his children. And since their marriage, the woman had borne him a third child, Florence was told.

When James Maybrick returned to Battlecrease House, Florence did not confront him, but acted as if everything were normal. Not that her husband would have noticed anyway. He began to stay out late, and often told Florence he would be going to London on business, but she found she could no longer trust him. She spent many interminable and lonely nights sitting alone in the drawing room, wondering where her husband really was. He had become a stranger to her. Then one night when he returned home late, she told him she could no longer sleep in the same bed as him.

In December 1888 the Maybricks were entertaining a number of guests at their home, one of whom viewed Florence with an amorous eye. He was a tall handsome 38-year-old bachelor named Alfred Brierley, a wealthy cotton broker who had offices in New Orleans and Liverpool, and who came from a prominent Lancashire family. Standing head and shoulders above the other guests, Brierley quickly caught the attention of Florence, who found him extremely charming.

Brierley was invited back many times and became a frequent dinner guest at the Maybrick house. During the following March Brierley often accompanied James and Florence Maybrick to the early spring horse races. As the weeks went by it was clear that Florence was becoming increasingly fond of Brierley, and vice versa. While James Maybrick was in London on business, Alfred Brierley visited Florence and declared his love for her. He asked her to go away with him. Florence tried to hold back her feelings for a while, then relented. She later spent three days with Brierley at Flatman's Hotel in London's Cavendish Square, posing as his wife.

Florence returned from her little sojourn on 28 March, and on the following day she accompanied her husband to Aintree for the Grand National. Among the crowd of racegoers was Alfred Brierley. Florence blushed and gave a tell-tale smile, which drove her husband wild with jealousy. To make matters worse, Brierley approached the Maybricks and asked Florence if she would like to see the Prince of Wales. Florence nodded and took his arm. The two smiled at each other under Florence's parasol as they made their way towards the grandstand.

Later that day at Battlecrease House, James Maybrick gave his wife a black eye during a fierce altercation over the Brierley incident, and Florence declared that enough was enough; she was leaving immediately. But James warned that if she did leave him, he would never allow her to see the children again. Florence walked to the hall, confused by her divided loyalties, and Maybrick roared, 'By heavens, Florrie, if you cross this doorstep you shall never enter this house again!' Reluctantly Mrs Maybrick turned on her heel and in tears was led by the children's nanny to the nursery where the baby was crying.

The following morning she sought the advice of the family physician, Dr Arthur Hopper. She told him of her husband's brutal attack on her, and, as Dr Hopper examined her black eye, she said she intended to see if a separation could be arranged. But the doctor tried to dissuade her, promising that he would drop in at Battlecrease House to confront Mr Maybrick about his deplorable behaviour.

About a week afterwards Alfred Brierley received a letter from Florence, urging him to visit her without delay. When Brierley arrived he was shocked to find that Florence had a black eye, and she told him about the beating she had received after returning home from the Grand National. Although visibly upset by the barbaric treatment Florence had received from her husband, he offered no remedy and no support whatsoever, which was another bitter blow to Florence.

On 13 April James Maybrick boarded a train for London, where he intended to spend the weekend with his brother, Michael, before consulting Dr Charles Fuller about the state of his health. Maybrick was something of a hypochondriac, and was continually preoccupied with the fear that every ache and pain heralded the onset of creeping paralysis. Ironically his few genuine health problems were caused by the arsenical medications he was forever taking for this imaginary disease.

Dr Fuller examined Maybrick and informed him that the symptoms he described indicated nothing more serious than dyspepsia, a mere stomach upset. Maybrick was very relieved to hear this, and returned to Liverpool in an optimistic mood on 22 April.

A couple of days after his return Florence Maybrick went to the local chemist shop of Thomas Wokes and bought a dozen fly-papers. She told the proprietor that the flies in her kitchen were getting out of hand. Mr

Wokes smiled, rolled up the fly-papers and handed them to the delivery boy. Mrs Maybrick paid him sixpence, then returned home, ahead of the delivery boy.

Several days later two servants were curious to see a towel covering something in Mrs Maybrick's room. One of them lifted the towel and saw a basin. In the basin was a small bowl also covered by a towel. This towel was lifted to reveal several fly-papers soaking in a bowl of water. In those days fly-papers contained significant amounts of arsenic; knowing this, the curious servants became quite suspicious. Two days later James Maybrick was coming downstairs when he experienced a distressing spell of dizziness. After the spell lifted, Maybrick proceeded to his office in the city. He arrived at the Knowsley Buildings shortly after 10.30am, and to his colleagues he complained of stiffness in the legs. That afternoon Maybrick tried to shake off his symptoms by going across the Mersey to watch the horse races on the Wirral. When he arrived his face was a sickly white, and several racetrack friends remarked that he looked quite unwell.

When Maybrick got home to Battlecrease House, he was sweating profusely. He went to bed, and when he awoke the next morning, he found his condition had not improved, so Doctor Humphreys, who was the children's doctor and the physician who lived nearest to the house, was summoned. When the doctor arrived, Mrs Maybrick told him about the white powder her husband had a habit of taking, and the doctor quizzed Maybrick about his arsenic addiction.

Later that day Mr Maybrick's condition improved slightly, and he was able to enjoy a bowl of oxtail soup. Maybrick's health was now on the mend, and by 30 April he no longer needed his wife to nurse him, so she took a break from her duties and attended a ball in Wavertree.

On Mayday James Maybrick was back to his usual self and seemed to have made a complete recovery – until he tried to eat. For the more he took food, the more nauseous he felt. Suddenly, on 3 May, Maybrick suffered a relapse, and his condition started to worsen to such an alarming extent, that Florence called for Dr William Carter, a prominent Rodney Street practitioner. When Dr Carter arrived, he was escorted to Mr Maybrick's bedroom and found his patient in a sorry state. Maybrick was writhing on the bed, double up from stomach pains, and had been vomiting. Dr Carter examined him and concluded that he was suffering from acute dyspepsia, but assured Florence that he would be as right as rain in a few days.

That same afternoon Alice Yapp, the children's nanny, spotted Florence pouring medicine from one bottle into another in a rather furtive manner. The nurse found this very suspicious, and on the following day decided to root through Mrs Maybrick's things. In a trunk belonging to her mistress, the nanny discovered a packet labelled 'arsenic'. This was the proof Nurse Yapp needed to confirm her suspicion. She immediately told Mrs Matilda Briggs, an old friend of Mr Maybrick, about the find. Then the motive behind the misdeed was discovered on the afternoon of 8 May, when Mrs Maybrick gave Nurse Yapp a letter to post. This letter was addressed to A. Brierley, Esq, 60 Huskisson Street, Liverpool. According to Nurse Yapp, on the way to the post office, she gave the letter to Mrs Maybrick's baby daughter, Gladys, and Gladys dropped the letter in some mud. As a result the nurse said she transferred the letter from the sullied envelope to a new clean one that she had bought from the post office earlier. In the process Nurse Yapp said she couldn't help noticing that Mrs Maybrick had described her husband's condition in the letter as 'sick unto death'.

Considering the fact that Mr Maybrick was only supposed to be suffering from dyspepsia, the phrase struck her as odd, to say the least. Nurse Yapp also noticed that Mrs Maybrick addressed Alfred Brierley as 'my own darling' in the letter.

Mrs Briggs told Mr Maybrick's brothers Edwin and Michael what she suspected, and the two men set off for Battlecrease House to investigate. When they arrived, Edwin showed his brother the letter that Nurse Yapp had opened. After a quick scan, Michael said, 'The woman is an adulteress.' When they went upstairs, they were shocked at the poor state of their brother. Michael visited Dr Humphreys' house that night and told him about the fly-papers in the bowl and how Nurse Yapp suspected Mrs Maybrick of poisoning her husband. But Dr Humphreys refused to take the allegation seriously.

At 8.30pm on 11 May, James Maybrick died, surrounded by his family and friends. But Florence was not there. Earlier that day, around 11am, she had fainted from the exhaustion brought on by the long hours spent at her sick husband's bedside and was lying in a semi-conscious state on the bed in the dressing room when Mr Maybrick expired.

Later that night Nurse Yapp discovered a brown paper parcel and a chocolate box. In the box were two bottles labelled 'arsenic', and the words, 'poison for cats' had been written on the label in red ink by someone. The brown paper parcel contained a yellowish powder. The brothers told a solicitor about the find, and he advised them to keep any evidence in a safe place, so they locked

70

the chocolate box and the parcel in the wine cellar.

Garston police were later notified, and were told that the circumstances surrounding Mr Maybrick's death were suspicious. An Inspector Baxendale soon turned up and interviewed the Maybrick brothers, Mrs Briggs and all of the servants, before viewing Mr Maybrick's body. Baxendale heard of their suspicions regarding Florence, and the next day, Michael Maybrick took the package of arsenic found by Miss Yapp from the locked cellar and handed it over to the inspector. That same day Superintendent Isaac Bryning instructed his men to take samples from the drains of Battlecrease House in case there were traces of arsenic lying in the sediments.

The revelations of the post-mortem that took place at five o'clock that afternoon strengthened the suspicions of the Maybrick brothers and Nurse Yapp. The lining of Maybrick's stomach was dappled with black patches, and the duodenum was scarlet with severe inflammation. Dr Alexander Barren, a professor of Pathology, and Dr Humphreys carried out the autopsy, and Dr Carter took notes throughout. Maybrick's stomach was removed and placed in a jar, which was sealed, then handed to Inspector Baxendale.

According to Dr Barren, Maybrick's death was due to acute inflammation of the stomach which in turn had been caused by an irritant poison.

On 14 May Florence Maybrick was arrested, taken to the local police station in Lark Lane, then escorted to Walton Gaol. A female warder took Mrs Maybrick's valuables, then led her to a cell in the prison's hospital.

The trial opened at St George's Hall on 31 July and lasted for seven days. The servants of Battlecrease House gave their damning evidence, as did Michael Maybrick and the various chemists who had innocently supplied Florence with her deadly doses of arsenic. And all this evidence was crowned by a Dr Stevenson, the Home Office expert on toxins, who stated categorically that Mr Maybrick had died of arsenic poisoning. And so, on the final day of the trial, at 3.56pm, the clerk of arraigns looked at the sombre jury and asked, 'Have you agreed upon a verdict, gentlemen?'

The foreman of the jury, a Mr Wainwright, replied, 'We have.'

'And do you find the prisoner guilty of the murder of James Maybrick or not guilty?'

'Guilty,' said Mr Wainwright, which brought forth a wave of sighs from the gallery.

Florence trembled slightly, and buried her face in her hands.

The clerk of arraigns turned to Florence and said, 'Florence Elizabeth Maybrick, you have been found guilty of wilful murder. Have you anything to say why the court should not pronounce sentence upon you?'

Florence rose from her seat in the dock and held the rail to steady herself. She bowed to his Lordship, then replied, 'My Lord, everything has been against me. Although evidence has been given as to a great many circumstances in connection with Mr Brierley, much has been withheld which might have influenced the jury had it been told. I am not guilty of this crime.'

Moments later the judge donned the black silk cap and read the death sentence. Sobs and sniffles from several women in the public gallery echoed through the court. Florence sat in the dock crying like a child.

When news of the verdict reached the huge crowd assembled outside St George's Hall, their hisses could be heard along the length of Lime Street. Later, when several servants who had given evidence emerged from St George's Hall, a rabble-rouser in the waiting throng mistakenly identified one of them as Nurse Yapp, and the crowd became agitated to such an extent that 70 policeman were summoned. As the servants were herded into a cab, the mob bombarded them with profanities. Later, when the judge that sentenced Mrs Maybrick left St George's Hall under a heavy police guard, the same wild crowd jeered at him and attacked the carriage into which he was rather keenly climbing. The carriage finally managed to escape from the thronged courtyard to a chant of 'Shame! Shame!'

About an hour later the crowd had still not disbanded, and mounted police had to be brought in to prepare the exit route for the prison van that was to take Florence Maybrick to the gallows at Walton Gaol. Florence was escorted to the van, and as soon as the vehicle started to move through the courtyard, a tremendous cheer swelled up, and did not fade until the van was lost from sight.

At Walton Gaol Florence was put into the condemned cell. The day of her execution was to be Monday, 26 August. Long before the dreaded date Florence heard only too well the terrifying sounds of sawing and hammering that signified the erection of the gallows.

But beyond the prison walls, an astounding turn of events was taking shape. A majority of the people in Britain and abroad thought that the Maybrick verdict was grossly unjust, and the Home Secretary was inundated with countless petitions for a reprieve. (The mere idea of a woman being hanged enraged many people in Victorian times.) But time was starting to run out.

Four days before the execution date, Florence was walking in Walton's prison yard when Mr Anderson, the governor of the gaol, called her name as he approached.

He said, 'Maybrick, no commutation of sentence has come down today, and I consider it is my duty to tell you to prepare for death.'

Florence replied, 'Thank you, governor. My conscience is clear. God's will be done.'

That night Florence Maybrick said her prayers and went to bed. At 1.30am she woke to the cacophony of wheels trundling over the courtyard outside. It was the cab of the Queen's messenger, who had come from London bearing good news. Moments later a key rattled in the lock of her cell door, and Florence sat up in bed, waiting anxiously. The prison governor entered with the chaplain and a warder. Florence listened in dreamy disbelief as the governor excitedly told her that she had been reprieved.

Florence's sentence was commuted to life imprisonment, and she spent 15 years as prisoner P29 in the gaols of Aylesbury and Woking, and did not enjoy freedom until July 1904. After her release Florence travelled to Rouen to be reunited with her mother, the Baroness von Roques. Towards the end of August that year Florence decided to return to the United States. Months after her emotional homecoming she wrote a book of her experiences in prison entitled, *My Fifteen Lost Years*.

Florence later dropped her famous (or should we say infamous) surname and replaced it with her maiden name, Chandler. Thereafer she shunned all publicity, becoming something of an eccentric recluse. She moved to Florida, then to Illinois, before finally spending her last days in an anonymous little shack among the woodlands of Connecticut.

In 1927 she made a final visit to Liverpool to attend the Grand National. On 24 October 1941 Florence was found dead in her little cabin. She was 79.

James Maybrick was 'revealed' to be Jack the Ripper in a diary that came to light in 1992. I believe the so-called *Diary of Jack the Ripper* to be a rather corny and badly-written fake, riddled with dozens of glaring errors. When news of the diary first emerged, Melvin Harris, a top expert on the Whitechapel Murders case, predicted that the book 'would be written in a journal or diary with a number of its front pages torn out'. Secondly, Harris forecast that it would be written in a simple iron-gall ink. This type of ink is indistinguishable from those used in the 1880s, but is easily made and not difficult to buy. Indeed some thousands of packets of ink-powder, once used in schools, are still around, and often turn up in street markets and antique shops. When mixed, it produces a Victorian-style ink. Melvin Harris was correct with both predictions. The diary looked like a journal or blank photographic album with a bunch of front-end pages suspiciously cut out. Mr Harris also stated that the ink showed traces of chloroacetamide – which was not used in inks until after the 1940s.

When I read the Diary, I found myself laughing at the numerous historical errors. For example, the diarist states: 'I took refreshment in the Poste House.' During Maybrick's life, the Poste House pub off Dale Street, was not called that – the pub was given that name in the 1980s - and there was not a single pub in the land called the Poste House in the 1880s. The diarist also states that, after butchering Mary Kelly, he left her breasts on the table. The official police files state categorically that one of the breasts was left by Kelly's right foot, and the other one was placed under her head. The diarist gets it wrong again when he says he regretted not taking any part of Kelly's body – but the actual Ripper had taken away the woman's heart – a fact suppressed by the police at the time, but which was only recently unearthed in Scotland Yard's files.

The diarist also repeats the common myth about the Ripper leaving rings and farthings at the feet of victim Annie Chapman, when the real Ripper took the woman's rings with him. Chapman didn't possess so much as a farthing at the time of her death. These are just a *few* of the many mistakes made in the diary. The writer of the diary says he has resorted to killing 'whores' as some sort of twisted revenge motive because of his wife's infidelities – but James Maybrick didn't even know his wife was having an affair with Alfred Brierley until *after* the five canonical Ripper murders had taken place!

Furthermore, the handwriting of the diary does not even bare the slightest resemblance to the Maybrick Will and other documents written in Maybrick's own hand. James Maybrick absolutely worshipped his children, so why would he want to leave behind a diary detailing his gruesome and cannibalistic work (because the Diary writer says he ate parts of the victims' wombs)? Such a diary would have forever besmirched the Maybrick children and cast a stain of notoriety against them forever more. People ignorant of these facts still make 'pilgrimages' to the grave of James Maybrick in Anfield Cemetery – a grave that was smashed in half by desecrators several years ago.

Did Florence Chandler really poison her husband? I believe she was innocent; so who *did* poison James Maybrick? Although Dr Stevenson, supposedly the

Home Office expert on toxins, stated categorically that Maybrick died of arsenical poisoning, a professor with a much greater knowledge of toxins – a Dr Rawdon MacNamara, Professor Materia Medica at the Royal College of Surgeons of Ireland, and the undisputed leading expert on arsenic in Europe, stated that Stevenson was wrong. The findings of Dr MacNamara suggested that James Maybrick had not died of arsenic poisoning at all, and therefore no murder had been committed. MacNamara was sure from the results of the Maybrick autopsy that the Aigburth cotton merchant had died of acute gastroenteritis.

There is no doubt in my mind that during the Maybrick murder trial, the more intelligent people in court realised that the Maybrick brothers, the Jannion sisters (two spinsters James Maybrick had once dated and jilted), and the servants of Battlecrease House had framed Florence to get her out of the way. The scheming brothers had convinced the dying James to cut his wife out of the will, and to hand the estate over to them. Edwin Maybrick even admitted that they had expected James to kill himself with his poisonous medications long before he became seriously ill. It is now also known that Justice Sir James Stephens, the judge who represented the crown during the seven-day trial, was not only confused because he was suffering from senile dementia, he was also obsessed with Florence Maybrick's extramarital affair, and accordingly steered the trial towards an interrogation of the woman's infidelities. This undoubtedly made the jury biased against Florence, and Sir Charles Russell, defending Mrs Maybrick, had to remind the court that she was on trial for a charge of murder – not adultery. Furthermore, the many affairs of

James Maybrick were not mentioned at all during the trial, illustrating the hypocritical double-standards of male society in Victorian times.

TWO VISIONS OF DEATH

Most people find the idea of assassination vile, and in Britain there is, fortunately, a remarkable shortage of Lee Harvey Oswalds, although on several occasions in the nation's history, prominent individuals have been disposed of for religious and political reasons. In December 1170 Thomas a Becket, the Archbishop of Canterbury, was assassinated by Hugh de Merville, William de Tracy, Reginal Fitzurse and Richard le Breton, four of Henry II's knights. Becket was callously slayed because of his opposition to Henry's attempts to control the clergy.

Assassinations of British prime ministers have been exceptionally scarce since the days of Walpole, and in almost three centuries of British politics, only one chief minister of government has been killed by an assassin. His name was Spencer Perceval, and the man who took his life was a Liverpudlian named John Bellingham.

Spencer Perceval was born in 1762, the second son of the second Earl of Egmont. He was educated at Harrow and Trinity College, Cambridge, where he graduated with a Master of Arts in 1781. In 1783 Perceval's mother, the Baroness Arden, died and left her fortune to her eldest son. Young Perceval struggled on, and studied hard to learn law at Lincoln's Inn. In 1786 he was called to the Bar, and soon obtained a reputation as a diligent and brief-hungry barrister. He also displayed a talent for voicing his strong political views, and in 1796 he entered Parliament as the Member for Northampton and became an ardent supporter of the Tory Prime Minister, William Pitt. When Henry Addington succeeded Pitt as premier in

1801, he persuaded Perceval to join the new government as attorney general. Perceval worked hard at his new job, and when Pitt formed his second administration in 1804, Perceval kept his job. In 1807 the Duke of Portland became Prime Minister in the House of Lords, and Spencer Perceval was made Chancellor of the Exchequer, and in those days that meant he was also the leader of the House of Commons. In 1809 King George III, who thought highly of the new leader of the Commons and once called him 'the most straightforward man I have ever known', asked him to become Prime Minister, and Perceval accepted.

In the spring of 1812, a 42-year-old bankrupt Liverpool insurance broker named John Bellingham entered a gunsmith's shop in the Strand, London, and bought two pistols and ammunition for four guineas. Bellingham left the shop and headed for the wide-open spaces of Primrose Hill for a bit of shooting practice, before returning to his lodgings in New Millman Street. Bellingham was a bitter and disillusioned man. He had once been involved in the lucrative business of exporting timber to Russia, but lost everything when a business contact went bankrupt. Unable to pay the resulting mammoth debts, Bellingham was thrown in prison. Upon his release, he visited Russia and complained to the authorities with such vigour that they imprisoned him too. Bellingham repeatedly wrote to the British ambassador to intervene on his behalf and secure his release, but the ensuing tangle of British and Soviet red tape achieved nothing, and Bellingham languished in a cold Russian prison cell for months.

When he was finally released, Bellingham returned to England and began a feverish campaign to get his case reviewed; he also demanded compensation. He wrote countless indignant letters to his MP and even informed the Prince Regent of his unjust incarceration. But all the protests came to nothing, and no redress was made. Once, Bellingham stormed into Whitehall and demanded action, but was met with a wall of unsympathetic officialdom. At the top of his voice he told one Whitehall official that he was going to take legal action against the government as a result of its wanton neglect; the official roared back, 'Go to the Devil!'

So John Bellingham decided to hit back at British bureaucracy by shooting the Prime Minister, preferably in the House of Commons and in the presence of all its members. But first he would have to do a bit of reconnoitring at the scene of the intended crime. Thereafter he made it his daily habit to visit the Commons, where he lurked about the central lobby, observing the route the Prime Minister took when entering the Chamber. He also became a frequent visitor to the Commons coffee room. And now for a strange supernatural twist to this tale ...

On the night of 3 May, a Mr John Williams, a wealthy banker of Scorrier House near Redruth, Cornwall, had a vivid dream in which he found himself standing in the lobby of the House of Commons. In this dream he saw a small man dressed in a blue coat and white waistcoat enter the lobby. Moments later, another man in a snuff-coloured coat with yellow metal buttons suddenly drew a small pistol and fired it at the man in blue. The dream was so realistic that the sleeping Mr Williams could actually discern the ball from the pistol striking the left side of the victim's chest, where it left a neat little spot. Shocked by the incident, the dreamer turned to a group of other people in the lobby and asked them who had been shot; someone replied that it was the Prime Minister, Spencer Perceval. The bystanders then charged at the murderer to apprehend him. At this point in the dream, Mr Williams awoke and gave an account of the strange dream to his wife. She assured him that it was just a dream, nothing else, and Mr Williams went back to sleep but the same disturbing dream replayed in his mind twice more that night.

On the following morning Mr Williams began to think about the significance of the recurring dream, and even wondered if he ought to travel to London to warn Mr Perceval. Later at work he related the previous night's events to several business acquaintances and asked them for advice. His friends told him that he would be ridiculed as a madman if he were to go to London on the strength of a mere dream, so he decided not to make the trip. All the same, he scanned *The Times* each day to see if there had been any shooting incidents at Westminster.

Unknown to John Williams, another person – who was never identified – had apparently also received a premonition of the Prime Minister's assassination a day or so before it took place, and this is attested in the pages of the *Dumfries and Galloway Courier* which reported that 'the Reverend Yorstoun, minister of Hoddam, had visited Kirk Bude and had obtained the most satisfactory proof of the rumour of the Prime Minister's assassination … on May 10th … but the rumour cannot be traced to its source.'

On the afternoon of Monday, 11 May, Spencer Perceval left 10 Downing Street and, seeing it was a nice sunny day, dismissed his carriage and set off to the House on foot. At around 5.15pm Perceval entered the lobby of the House, and a few seconds later Bellingham drew his pistol from his right-hand breeches pocket. He stepped out from behind a pillar, raised his pistol, aimed it at Perceval, and in full view of all the constituents, he fired. The ball blasted a small neat hole in the left side of the Prime Minister's chest. Perceval cried, 'Murder!' and staggered three paces; then he fell on his side and rolled face down on to the floor. Mr Goodiff, an officer of the House attacked the assassin, grabbed his arm and restrained him. He asked Bellingham if he had shot the Prime Minister, and Bellingham replied, 'I am the unhappy man who has shot Mr Perceval. My name is John Bellingham. I know what I have done. It was a private injury, a denial of justice on the part of the government.'

Bellingham was instantly recognised by Sir Banastre Tarleton and Mr Gascoyne, two Liverpool MPs who were in the Lobby at the time. Gascoyne also sprang upon Bellingham and twisted his arm, while someone removed the smoking pistol from his hand. The assassin was then body-searched, and the second pistol was found on him.

Meanwhile Perceval was carried into the nearby office of the Speaker's secretary and laid on a sofa. When Doctor Lynn of Great Smith Street arrived ten minutes later, he found he could do nothing. Perceval was dead.

All the doors of the House were locked and Bellingham was taken along several private passages to the prison rooms in the upper storey of the Commons, where he was interrogated by the Cabinet Council for over seven hours.

Perceval's body was later taken to his wife and five children, who were, of course, absolutely devastated by the killing.

News of the murder travelled quickly across the nation, and there were many in the upper echelons of British society who believed that the assassination was but the starting shot of the long-awaited British Revolution. Paranoid aristocrats shuddered, recalling the Revolution across the channel in France that had occurred a mere two decades earlier. The social unrest among the poverty-stricken lower classes, fuelled by the introduction of machines into the workplace, seemed ready to explode any day, and the riotous activities of the Luddites were becoming increasingly organised. To make matters worse, the country's economy was at an all-time low because of the cost of the Napoleonic Wars. But one individual who learned of the assassination was more dumbfounded than shocked. He was Mr Williams of Cornwall, the man who had foreseen the shooting in a recurring dream. He immediately travelled to London, and purchased a tinted etching of the Prime Minister's murder, and was astounded to see that every detail of the drawing was identical to the details he had witnessed in his dream — from the colours of the coats to the exact position of the gunshot wound in the victim's chest.

Following his interrogation in the House, Bellingham was taken under a strong guard of Dragoons to a waiting hackney coach in the Lower Palace Yard outside. By this time the crowds had swelled, and when they saw the tall gaunt figure of Bellingham, they shouted 'Burdett for ever!'

The mob was referring to Sir Francis Burdett, a popular politician of the time who had been imprisoned for advocating freedom of speech, Catholic emancipation, and other liberal measures. As Bellingham entered the coach, several of the more daring members of the crowd attempted to give him a chance of escape by trying to prise open the opposite door of the carriage, but a party of Life Guards suddenly arrived and formed a semicircle around the coach. Moments later, the coach trundled off across the yard and made its way to Newgate Prison.

Bellingham was tried on 15 May and it took the jury only 15 minutes to return a verdict of guilty. He was sentenced to death by hanging, and while he waited for the 18th, his execution date, he sat in his cell writing letters to his wife in Duke Street, Liverpool, assuring her that he would be coming home in a day or two.

On the Monday morning of 18 May at 7.20, the Lord Mayor, Sheriffs and a 20-strong crowd of other notables arrived at Newgate to see the sentence of law executed. The usual throng of necrophiles and various sensation-seekers looked on from window seats and rooftops overlooking the gallows – indeed any vantage point that afforded a decent view of the execution scene. At 7.30am Bellingham came down from his cell with the Reverend Doctor Ford to have his irons knocked off. The two men were then joined by the Mayor and Sheriffs, and they all walked into the press yard where the condemned had to wait in the rain until he was instructed to approach the scaffold. Shortly afterwards Bellingham's wrists were tied together, and a rope tied around both arms at waist level. At this point a tear trickled down the condemned man's face, and he told the executioner to make the noose tight to ensure 'no inconvenience'. He ascended the steps of the scaffold with the priest, and some members of the crowd started shouting 'Hurrah!' But a far greater number retorted by shouting 'Silence!'

The rope was fastened around Bellingham's neck and the white cap was placed on his head. At this point the priest started to pray with Bellingham for a while, then asked him how he felt. Calmly and rationally Bellingham said he thanked God for having enabled him to meet his fate with so much fortitude and resignation.

The executioner put the white linen hood over his head and Bellingham objected. But Reverend Ford told him he would have to wear it. The hood was tied around the lower part of Bellingham's face with a white handkerchief. The crowd started to chant 'God bless you' over and over, then a terrible hush descended on the scene. The executioner stepped down below the scaffold and got ready to strike away the supports of the trapdoor on which Bellingham was standing. The clock struck 8am, and on the seventh chime, the executioner removed the supports with one skilful blow, and John Bellingham dropped. His death was swift, because the executioner had decided to pull on the hanged man's legs to speed the process of neck-breaking strangulation.

The body, with its grotesquely dislocated and elongated neck, was left to hang until 9am, when it was cut down, swung on to a cart and covered with a sack. The executioner's assistant and a boy took the cart to St Bartholomew's Hospital, where it was first disembowelled and then thoroughly dissected before a ghoulish gaggle of public spectators.

One hundred and sixty-eight years later another assassination took place, but this time a Liverpool man was not the assassin, but the victim, and this killing was also said to have been foreseen.

On 8 September 1980, an American psychic named Alex Tanous was being interviewed by Lee Spiegel for NBC radio's *Unexplained Phenomena Show*. The interview was going out live and was being held in the office of the

American Society for Psychical Research, which is located on West 73rd Street in New York City.

Spiegel asked Tanous to prove his alleged powers of second sight by making a prediction, preferably one that would be of particular interest to the radio station's audience, who belonged to the 18-35 age group. Tanous paused for a moment, as if concentrating, then said, 'A very famous rock star will have an untimely death, and this can happen from this moment on. I say "untimely" because there is something strange about this death, but it will affect the consciousness of many people because of his fame. The star will be foreign-born but living in the United States.' After giving his prediction, Tanous glanced through the windows of his office at the building opposite, a superior high-rise known as the Dakota Apartments.

Three months later, on the night of 8 December, a limousine pulled up outside the Dakota Apartments building at 10.50pm, and Yoko Ono left the vehicle. Her husband John Lennon followed her a few moments later, clutching several reels of tape from a recording session on which he'd been working. As John walked under the archway leading to the Dakota building, he heard a voice behind him call out, 'Mr Lennon'.

John turned to see tubby 25-year-old Mark Chapman a mere 20 feet away, crouched in a combat stance and pointing a .38 Undercover Special handgun. A heartbeat later Chapman pumped four hollow-point bullets into one of Liverpool's most famous and adored sons. The songwriter who urged the world's leaders to 'give peace a chance' staggered up the steps of the building's entrance and fell flat on his face. Minutes later John was placed on the back seat of a police car which rushed him to the nearest hospital with its roof-lights flashing and its siren screaming. As the police car jumped the traffic lights on Broadway, police officer James Moran, who had been a Beatles fan in his youth, leaned back and talked to John Lennon in a vain attempt to keep him conscious. Moran was deeply shocked at the shooting, but to his dying idol he managed to say, 'Are you John Lennon?'

With his life rapidly ebbing away, John faintly replied, 'Yes.'

And that was the last word John Lennon uttered. He was the 701st person to be gunned down in New York City that year.

Chapman is currently serving a '20 years to life' sentence at Attica Correctional Facility just outside of Buffalo, New York. He was originally kept in solitary confinement to prevent any of the prison's other inmates from attacking him, but now ventures out of his cell to carry out housekeeping and library work. He has been denied parole six times, but is entitled to re-apply for parole every two years because he has served over 25 years in prison. A parole hearing board has deemed that Lennon's sons, as well as Yoko Ono, and Chapman himself would be at risk if he was allowed parole.

Chapman's motive for killing the ex-Beatle is still unclear. The official theory was that Chapman was simply a psychotic Lennon fanatic trying to make a name for himself, but there is something more sinister about the killing. Chapman was dismissed as a 'lone nut' - the same expression that was used to describe Lee Harvey Oswald 17 years earlier in Dallas, Texas. In fact the murder of John Lennon has several striking parallels with that of John F Kennedy. When Lennon's body was taken to the morgue, the gunshot wounds in the cadaver were so close together that one pathologist remarked, 'Good shot group' – which is a firing-range term used by the police and the military to describe skilled marksmanship. Yet Chapman was said to be a novice with firearms. But the grouping of the gunshot wounds in Lennon's body was so tight that pathologists at the morgue got mixed up trying to count them as they conducted their post-mortem.

The assassin's choice of weapon, the Undercover Special, known on the street as a 'Saturday night special', is an extremely reliable gun. It is deadly accurate and very rarely jams or misfires, yet is small and sleek enough to fit into the back pocket of your jeans. In May 1972 would-be assassin Arthur Bremner used one to blast Alabama Governor George C Wallace. The bullet that impacted into the politician's spine left him wheelchair-bound for life.

Besides the mystery of Chapman's expert choice of weapon and his inexplicable marksmanship, there is the fuzzy account of the killer's journey from his home in Honolulu to New York that just doesn't stand up to the most cursory examination. According to the official version of events, Mark Chapman persuaded his wife to take out a loan of $2,500 from her employer's credit union, and without her knowledge he used this sum to finance the assassination. He bought his well-chosen gun and dum-dum bullets, and flew overnight from Honolulu to New York on a United Airlines plane. But the late distinguished British barrister Fenton Bresler, who researched the Lennon murder for eight years, unearthed a plethora of sinister missing links. Firstly, he discovered that United Airlines had no direct flights from Honolulu to New York. One actually had to fly by way of Chicago. Chapman did not mention this. Further investigations made by Bresler convinced the barrister that the killer spent three unaccounted-for days in Chicago. Bresler got in touch with the New York County district attorney's office and told them about the three 'missing' days, but they denied that the facts had any substance. Bresler believes that the days in question — from the 2nd to the 5th of December – were covered up by the authorities. During that period, he claims, Chapman was probably being 'programmed' to kill by the CIA with brainwashing drugs and repeated hypnotic suggestion. Is Bresler right? Was there a top-level conspiracy to assassinate John Lennon? Let us examine some less-publicised facts about one of Liverpool's most famous sons.

The FBI and the CIA had files on Lennon dating back to the 1960s that detail the star's participation in anti-war demos. There are two reports in one dossier on Lennon for May 1972 with the heading 'Revolutionary Activities'. The FBI and CIA apparently saw Lennon as a cult-like leader who had the latent ability to overthrow the established government of the United States; a political subversive who could easily produce a song along the lines of 'Power to the People' to incite millions of Americans to demonstrate against the reactionary policies of the newly-elected president Ronald Reagan. As early as 1972 Lennon knew he was under constant surveillance. He said at the time to reporters, 'I'd open the door. There'd be guys on the other side of the street. I'd get into my car, and they'd be following me in a car. Not hiding. They wanted me to see that I was being followed.'

By September 1973 Lennon's telephone was bugged, a fact to which even the Justice Department later admitted. In December 1975 Lennon said, 'We knew we were being wire-tapped. There was a helluva lot of guys coming in to fix the phones.'

In the light of these cloak-and-dagger details, Bresler's conspiracy theory seems less outlandish. Furthermore, the week John Lennon was shot he was due to fly to San Francisco to participate in a rally for Japanese-American workers on strike. He was so enthusiastic to get to the demonstration, he had already bought the airline tickets.

In November 1992 Mark Chapman broke his silence over the Lennon murder when he agreed to be interviewed by American television reporter Barbara Walters in Attica State prison. Chapman dismissed the commonly held belief that he had killed John Lennon to become famous. He also told Walters that he was horrified by the amount of fan-mail he regularly received from people wanting his autograph.

'That tells you something is truly sick in our society,' Chapman told Walters in a broken voice.

MORPHINE AND MATRIMONY

In 1904 a handsome young man named Robert Clements graduated from Queen's University in Belfast. He was a gifted conversationalist and had a charismatic aura about him. He specialised in gynaecology, but he was also a surgeon and physician, and he was also something of a Romeo. Clements had no shortage of young female admirers, and yet the good doctor married a plain-looking woman ten years his senior, and everybody suspected that Clements had only married her because she was the daughter of a wealthy miller.

Two years after receiving £25,000 from her father in 1918, Clements' wife fell ill and later died, intestate, with a mere £10 left in her savings. Before her relatives could find out where the rest of her fortune had disappeared to, Mr Clements took a trip across the Irish Sea and settled in Moss Side, Manchester, where he met and married a beautiful young colleen from County Antrim, who also suspiciously died five years later. Dr Clements signed the death certificate himself and stated the cause of death as endocarditis, then promptly transferred the £425 his second wife had left him into his bank account.

In 1928 Kathleen Burke succumbed to Clements' charm and became wife number three. After eleven years of marriage Kathleen died quite suddenly one day at their Southport home, and the widowed Dr Clements again benefited from the death of a spouse. Kathy left him £489 in her will. The police suspected that the death of this third wife might not be a product of coincidence. They quickly telephoned the Liverpool Crematorium and gave the order to halt the incineration of Mrs Clements' body so that the corpse could be examined to see if it contained any traces of poison. But the call from the police came at the precise moment when Mrs Clements was being consumed by fire.

Undaunted by the police's suspicions, the audacious Dr Clements was soon seen walking hand in hand with the young porcelain-skinned Amy Victoria Barnett, the girl he had been seeing behind his late wife's back. Amy was the daughter of an immensely rich Lancashire magnate who wanted nothing but the best for his little girl, so he financed the grand wedding at St George's, in London's Hanover Square.

After the honeymoon the couple settled down in their luxurious, semi-detached Southport home. Mr and Mrs Clements were well liked by their neighbours and attended the nearby Christ Church without fail every Sunday morning. But married life turned sour for the Clements. Amy seemed to go cold, and on many occasions the doctor returned home to find that his carefree wife had not even bothered to cook him a meal.

When Mrs Clements died suddenly in May 1947, Dr J M Houston, the pathologist who performed the post-mortem, recorded the cause of death as myeloid leukaemia. The West Lancashire coroner was quick to act this time, and he despatched two detectives to cancel the funeral. Two Home Office forensic experts, Dr W H Grace and Dr J B Firth, were called in to examine the body. But the doctors discovered that a kidney and several other organs were absent from the deceased woman. They had been removed by Dr Houston during the post-mortem and burned. So Dr Firth made a painstaking analysis of the remaining kidney and discovered one-third of a grain of morphine in it. He then carefully took several samples from the spinal column and took them to his Preston laboratory. For a week Firth subjected the vertebrae samples to every known chemical screening process – and discovered one-twentieth of a grain of morphine. Amy Victoria Clement had been murdered.

Morphine crystals were also found in a hypodermic syringe belonging to Dr Clements, and the same drug was found in tablet form in a bottle labelled 'phenobarbitone'.

But the proof of murder came too late; Dr Clements was found dead at his home. A squirt of morphine from his syringe was the means of committing his *felo de se*.

It was a simple task for the jury to decide that the doctor had killed his last wife, but as the murderer had committed suicide there was no way of proving that the doctor had also killed his three previous wives, although it seems very likely that this was the case. If he did kill all of his wives, was it greed that drove the doctor to the despicable deeds? Or was he one who simply loathed the mind-numbing ennui of his marriages, and longed for a change of routine? This does seem to be the case, as shortly before his suicide, the doctor told a friend, 'I cannot remember when I ate a cooked meal in my own flat.'

There was an eerie instance of murder repeating itself regarding the case of the murderous Doctor Clements. Between 1975 and 1998, another doctor named Harold Shipman, killed at least 218 patients, mostly using a form of morphine known as diamorphine (commonly known as heroin). Like Dr Clements, Shipman was above suspicion, being a doctor – until another doctor thought it strange how Shipman had amassed so many forms authorising the cremation of deceased patients. These suspicions eventually reached the ears of the police, but the investigating officers could find insufficient evidence of foul play at first. The last victim of Shipman was an 81-year-old woman who had died – supposedly of old age – according to Shipman. This woman also just happened to have left Shipman £386,000 in her will. Police later found the typewriter that had been used to type up that highly-suspect will – it was in the possession of Harold Shipman, of course.

On 31 January 2000, Harold Fredrick Shipman was found guilty of just 15 of the 218 murders he was suspected of committing, and he was sentenced to what is known as the 'whole life tariff' whereby a prisoner is to spend his or her entire life behind bars until they die.

Shipman hanged himself in his cell at Wakefield Prison, West Yorkshire, on 13 January 2004.

THE ELIZABETH PEERS MURDER MYSTERY

I have studied the paranormal for many years, and have come to the conclusion that some ghosts are undoubtedly 'impressions' left by a traumatic event. The following haunting is a case in point.

In the 1980s, a ghostly girl in a cloak was allegedly seen on many occasions walking down Liverpool's Lodge Lane and several of the nearby streets between Edge Hill and Toxteth. I knew someone who claimed he had seen the phantom girl, and he was not a man who was known to lie or tell fanciful tales. He had no interest in ghosts, or any aspect of the paranormal and had rather a shallow, pragmatic philosophy of life which left no room for the supernatural. It was a surprise to his wife, therefore, when she heard him screaming her name as he hammered on the front door of his home one evening in 1982.

The man, John, lived at a house on Scholar Street at the time, and he'd been returning from the nearby Boundary pub on the corner of Lodge Lane and Smithdown Road when he saw the apparition. It was a little after 11pm, and there was a light drizzle. One person – an old man – passed him, and John thought Smithdown Road was unusually quiet, even for a midweek night. All of a sudden he saw the eerie-looking figure of a girl, aged about twelve, he reckoned. She wore a beret and a long cloak, and her face was a deathly white, as were her small hands. Her eyes were huge black and lifeless as a doll's. She walked slowly towards him, her mouth open, making a low moaning sound. John felt the hairs on the back of his neck stand on end, and goose-pimples simultaneously rose on his arms. He just knew that the sinister-looking child was not a living child, but some phantasm of a dead person. He ran all the way to his home, too afraid to look back. That night he hugged his wife tightly in bed till the pale light of dawn filtered through the bedroom curtains, and the couple heard the distinct sounds of a child crying somewhere outside until around 3am.

The ghost John had encountered was seen a few days later, this time by a man on his way to work at around 6.30 in the morning. The description was the same, and the man described the beret John had seen as a tam o'shanter. Like John, this second witness was spooked by the pallid-faced apparition, and he hurried down Longfellow Street in a state of fright, glancing back over his shoulder several times to see if the ghost was following. It wasn't. The apparition stood on the corner, motionless.

These reports continued for a while, and then the ghost made itself increasingly scarce. It's still occasionally seen, but nowhere as frequently as it was in the 1980s. I decided to research the case, and unearthed a very tragic but mysterious tale. Back in the year 1905, the Peers family lived at 64 Wendell Street, off Smithdown Road. The family had originally lived on Bective Street, off Earle Road, but had moved to Wendell Street around 1902. The head of the family was 47-year-old William Peers, a bricklayer by trade. He and his 43-year-old wife Elizabeth had five sons and a beautiful, intelligent ten-year-old daughter, also named Elizabeth.

Around midnight on Saturday, 28 October 1905, Mrs Peers sent her daughter to a butcher's shop on Lodge Lane for some cooked pork. The child was given sixpence and a plate to carry the pork home, and so she set off on her errand. In that day and age, the junction of Smithdown Road and Lodge Lane formed part of a thickly populated neighbourhood, where the shops stayed open later than usual on Saturday nights, and the electric tramcars continued to run after midnight. Elizabeth wore a smart dress, a long cloak, and a tam o'shanter on her head, and presented quite a pretty sight. She walked off from her home in Wendell Street and headed down Longfellow Street towards Lodge Lane.

Elizabeth Peers never returned from her errand.

Mrs Peers had a married brother who lived nearby, and sometimes Elizabeth went to see him, and so when the child didn't return from the butcher's by one in the morning, Mrs Peers assumed she was at her uncle's. However, the hours wore on, and soon Mrs Peers and her husband John began to worry for their child's safety. They hoped and prayed nothing had happened to her, and they got in contact with relatives who told them that Elizabeth was not staying with her uncle. What then, had become of her?

On the following morning, a Sunday, at 8.35am, a little eight-year-old girl named Frances Myles who had been sent to fetch a jug of milk from a local shop skipped through the entry that backed on to Cullen Street – just three streets along from Wendell Street – when she came across a girl laying on her back. The little girl didn't properly take in the ghastly scene, but simply went home and babbled something about a girl who had fainted in the entry. The girl's mother took no notice. Meanwhile, a young carter named Bill Wilson, came out of his backyard, on his way to work at a local stable, and noticed something on the ground in the gloomy entry. At first he thought it was a bundle of tarpaulin, but when he stooped and examined the object, he saw it was a beautiful girl lying on her back. She was wearing some sort of cloak, which had been uncoupled from around her neck and placed under her body. A tam o'shanter the girl had worn was lying nearby. The girl had one arm raised in a peculiar grotesque way, for that arm had been deformed and twisted out of shape as if something heavy had crushed it. The girl looked to be about nine or ten years of age, and her eyes were wide open, each under a puddle of rain in its socket, as was her mouth which had also filled with rainwater, and she was obviously dead.

Her face bore an expression of extreme shock. Her skin was pale as snow and there were strange small black bruises on her face. The stunned and sickened carter also noticed bruising on the child's throat, as if the girl had been strangled. The flesh on one side of her face looked swollen, as if someone had hit her hard. The body was soaked through by the downpour that had lasted from three in the morning. The carter raised the alarm, and the body was carried to a nearby house, where resuscitation was attempted but quickly found to be a waste of time. The child was dead and beyond all medical help. The body was taken to the Southern Hospital, where doctors officially pronounced life extinct.

The Peers family feared the worst when they heard about the girl's body being found in the entry, and they later identified their child. It was Elizabeth. On 31 October, a post mortem examination revealed that the child had been violently raped. She had died from suffocation and shock to her genitals, caused by being simultaneously choked and raped by person or persons unknown. On Friday 3 November at 3pm, Elizabeth Peers was buried at Toxteth Park Cemetery on Smithdown Road. An incredible thirty thousand people attended the funeral, conducted by the Vicar of St Clement's Church. After the burial service, the vicar said an outrage had undoubtedly been committed in open defiance of the Commandments. The vicar said Heaven was angry with the wicked man who had perpetrated the foul deed, and that God had sharpened his sword against him. One of the many touching floral tributes adorning the coffin and graveside was a wreath from Tiber Street School, which Elizabeth Peers had attended. A smaller wreath was from a playmate from this school, and the violets simply formed the name 'Lizzie'.

The murderer of Elizabeth Peers was said to have been glimpsed by several witnesses that night, and to me he seems rather familiar, but more on that later. Mr G A Wolstenholme, was returning to his home that night after a trip to Widnes, and when he reached the corner of Cullen Street, between 1.15am and 1.20am, he saw a man coming out of the back entry of Cullen Street, looking alarmed and agitated. He was around 35 to 40 years of age, about 5 feet 10 inches in height and sported a dark moustache. Another witness saw this same man earlier that night at 11.15pm, close to the murder scene. The police subsequently discovered that the killer had taken Elizabeth Peers into an empty house on Cullen Street and murdered her before taking the body outside into the entry. The killer placed the plate Elizabeth had been given to carry the pork home, close to her body. The sixpence the girl had carried to buy the pork was never accounted for, and was possibly pocketed by the murderous rapist.

The murderer of Elizabeth Peers was never brought to justice, but it is just possible that the Liverpool police unwittingly interviewed him while they were conducting their investigation of the crime. Police investigative procedures have changed dramatically since Edwardian times, and had Lizzie Peers been murdered today, detectives would have scrutinised the testimony and background of any person who claimed to have been in close proximity of the murder scene within minutes of the murder. Cast your mind back to the previous paragraph – to the testimony of Mr G A Wolstenholme – George Amos Wolstenholme to give him his full name.

George was a dock labourer, living at 41a St Anne Street – a lodging house kept by a Mrs Catherine James. He had lived on and off at the lodging house for twelve months, but had been a regular lodger for the three months prior to the murder of Elizabeth Peers. George A Wolstenholme had a clear recollection of his movements on the day of the murder, so he told police after volunteering information at Derby Road police station after hearing of the Smithdown Road murder. Wolstenholme said he had been in the vicinity of the scene of the Peers murder on the night it had occurred, and what's more, Wolstenholme described a suspicious-looking man hurrying away from the very alleyway where the little girl's body would be found. However, at the inquest into the Peers murder, before coroner, T E Sampson, Wolstenholme told a convoluted and apparently contradictory story to explain how he had come to be on Smithdown Road between 1.15am and 1.30am. 'I went to Widnes that day [28 October 1905] between noon and a little after 1pm,' the dock labourer told the coroner, 'and I got to Widnes at 1.20pm. I went there with a man named Harry Smith, a docker like myself, and we asked around a few public houses for a man named Thompson, from whom we hoped to get work. But we were told that Thompson had left, so we decided to leave Widnes at seven o'clock, and having no money, we walked back to Liverpool.'

According to Wolstenholme, by 1am, he and his friend Smith had reached Smithdown Road after a five and a half hour walk, and as they neared the workhouse (where the Asda supermarket now stands) Smith stopped, saying his feet were too sore to continue, so Wolstenholme left him there and walked on. He went up an alleyway off Cullen Street (which is just a few hundred yard from Wendell Street, where Elizabeth Peers lived) to urinate. The time was now between 1.15am and 1.30am. Wolstenholme then saw an entry on his left, and from this alleyway, a dark-haired man emerged at a brisk pace, in an alarmed and agitated state, according to the docker. The stranger was between 35 to 40 years of age, about 5 feet 10 inches in height, and of stout build. He sported a dark moustache, and he wore a dark cap, a muffler scarf round his neck, a dark coat and vest, and moleskin trousers which looked as if they had been splashed with dirty water from the thighs downwards.

'Which way did he go?' the coroner asked.

'He went into Smithdown Road and turned round towards Tunnel Road,' replied Wolstenholme.

'Do you think you could identify this man if you saw him again?' asked the coroner.

Wolstenholme nodded. 'Yes, sir. I was only five yards away from him at the time and he passed near a lamp-post. There was no one else about though.'

'Where did you go after seeing him?' queried the coroner.

'I went down Crown Street, on to London Road, past the Old Haymarket, and then I went up Stanley Road to the Alexandra Dock, because I had heard there was work on a boat there, but this wasn't the case, so I then went home to my lodgings. I got back there, in St Anne Street, about seven in the morning. No one saw me go into the lodging house and I went straight to bed.'

On Monday, Wolstenholme read of the sickening rape and murder of Elizabeth Peers off Smithdown Road, and shuddered when he read the part of the article which said the girl had been found in an alleyway at the back of Cullen Street – the very alleyway in which Wolstenholme had urinated after his epic walk from Widnes, and he immediately thought about that man he had seen hurrying from the alleyway. The dock labourer therefore went to the police a few days later and told them what he had seen.

A Mr Duder, acting on behalf of the Liverpool Police, cross-examined Wolstenholme, and poked many holes in his testimony. 'I put it to you,' Duder told the witness, 'that you did not go from Central Station that day.'

'Yes I did,' retorted Wolstenholme with a puzzled look.

'You went to Widnes from Central Station on a train, leaving after one?' asked Duder.

'Yes,' said Wolstenholme.

'There was no train!' exclaimed Duder, and he continued: 'There is a train at 12.33pm and one at 1.30pm that does not stop at Widnes – and the next train that stops at Widnes is the 1.50pm. So, do you still say you left by train?'

'I know it was a train sir,' Wolstenholme told him, 'and I believe it was the Central Station. I am not sure, for the simple reason I had a drop of drink in me at the time.'

'When did you pay your landlady the rent for your lodgings that day?' Duder asked.

'In the afternoon,' replied Wolstenholme.

'How could you pay in the afternoon if you were in Widnes?' Duder asked. 'Was she at Widnes as well?'

'No,' was Wolstenholme's flat-sounding response.

'So, you did pay her?' sighed Duder, 'That part of the story is true? And the story of your going to Widnes is not true?'

'Yes sir,' was Wolstenholme's vague reply.

'How can they both be true?' roared Duder. 'Try and recollect and tell the truth! You are bothering everybody, as they can't speak out plain!'

Wolstenholme began to perspire, and a nervous tic played in his face.

Duder shook his head, and then apologised to the witness for shouting at him in such a manner, but asked him again to give coherent unambiguous answers.

Wolstenholme bowed his head in the witness box and examined his hands.

Duder addressed the witness again. 'Now, I put it to you that there *is* a train from Lime Street to Widnes which departs at 1.20pm. This train does not leave from Central Station. Now, once again, I ask you: what time of day did you pay the money to Mrs James, your landlady?'

'Between one o'clock and half-past one, because I was paid early that day,' said Wolstenholme, confidently.

The coroner, Mr Sampson, interposed at this point, and questioned Wolstenholme with an expression of incredulity: 'If you went to Widnes on the one twenty pm train, then you simply could not have paid your landlady between one pm and one thirty pm.'

'I was paid my wages at the Canada Dock at one o'clock sir,' Wolstenholme replied, 'And when I left the lodging house, I had just three shillings in my pocket, so I must have paid her. I then set off to find work from a man named Thompson in Widnes.'

'And then you returned to Liverpool because you, and a Mr Smith, failed to find Thompson?' the coroner asked.

'Yes sir,' affirmed Wolstenholme, 'and it rained heavily as we walked back, so we were soaked through by the time we reached Smithdown Road Workhouse, where Mr Smith and I parted company.'

'And as you were in the vicinity of Cullen Street you noticed the man you described earlier?' queried the coroner.

'Yes sir,' replied the witness.

'And what made you take such particular notice of him?' the coroner asked.

'Well, because he seemed to be in such a hurry,' said Wolstenholme.

'And in this short time while he was walking past the lamp you took in all these details? Even the colour of his hair?' coroner Sampson asked.

'Yes sir,' replied Wolstenholme.

The coroner pitched another question at the difficult witness. 'And on the following Monday, you told John Thompson about this at the lodging house?'

'Yes sir.'

'And what did you tell him?' asked Sampson.

'I don't remember,' was woolly-minded Wolstenholme's reply.

'Well, what time of the day was this?' asked the patient coroner.

'I have no idea,' claimed Wolstenholme.

'Were your clothes clean on the Saturday night [the night of the murder]?' asked the coroner.

'Yes sir.'

'And on the Sunday and Monday?'

'Yes.'

The coroner then asked Wolstenholme: 'And, you had no need to wash the clothes then?'

'No, sir,' Wolstenholme replied, but seemed rather uneasy.

'Then why did you wash them?' the coroner asked. The landlady of Wolstenholme's lodging-house had told the coroner in her statement that Wolstenholme had washed his clothes after the murder.

Wolstenholme had an answer for the coroner. 'I washed my clothes because I wanted to pawn my shirt. In a lodging-house we have to wash our clothes when we get the chance; there are so many wanting to wash their clothes.'

'Are you in lodgings now?' Sampson asked.

'No sir,' replied the dock labourer, 'I am in the Brownlow Hill Workhouse Hospital, because I am ill. I wasn't ill when I was walking back from Widnes that night, but I am ill now.' Wolstenholme did not specify what his illness was to the court, but had told his landlady a week before that he was going into the workhouse because he had a sore leg which had been injured years before when he fought in South Africa.

The man Wolstenholme said he had walked from Widnes with – Harry Smith, a docker working in the Alexandra Dock – was traced by the police and brought to the court, but Mr Smith had not only been working on a ship on the day of the supposed trip to Widnes, he had never set eyes on George Amos Wolstenholme in his life, and as far as Smith knew, there was no other Harry Smith who worked in the Alexandra Dock. Smith also cast grave doubts on Wolstenholme's claim about the way his wages were paid. 'Dockers are never paid before two o'clock on a Saturday afternoon,' Smith said.

Catherine James, the 51-year-old landlady of the lodging-house on St Anne Street, stated on oath that her lodger George Wolstenholme had not been working on the day of the murder, Saturday, 28 October. She distinctly remembered that he had been about the lodging-house that day and she had seen him on several occasions, and she recalled that, between 3.30pm and 4pm, he had paid her two shillings and fourpence for the week's lodgings – and then he had gone out and she hadn't see him until the Sunday afternoon when she went to make his bed and found him asleep in it. A few days later, Wolstenholme said to the landlady, 'Listen, if two detectives call here, you're to tell them I live here.'

When the detectives did call, Mrs James overheard Wolstenholme telling them that he had been in the neighbourhood of Cullen Street when the little girl had been murdered. After the detectives left, the landlady naturally asked her lodger what he'd been doing in the area of the murder that night, and Wolstenholme claimed that he had gone to visit a friend, but when he had seen the attic windows of his friend's house wide open, he had realised that he must have long since left the dwelling – but Wolstenholme would not tell her what street this friend had lived in. Mrs James then told him she had heard him tell the detectives that he had gone down the entry into Cullen Street, and Wolstenholme said that was true – he had. 'Then surely you would have seen that poor little girl's body laying there?' Mrs James asked him.

'No,' replied Wolstenholme, 'she might have been twenty or thirty yards further up the alleyway.'

The landlady also told the court how she had found a shirt and a piece of rag under her lodger's mattress and Wolstenholme had never explained why he had stuffed the items under his mattress.

John Thompson, aged 42, introduced to the court as a kitchen man who worked in Mrs James's lodging-house, gave his testimony regarding Wolstenholme's story. The first question posed by the coroner could never be asked in a court today: 'Is Wolstenholme right in the head?'

To which Thompson replied, 'He acts very foolishly sometimes.'

'Is he fond of teasing children?' the coroner asked.

'Well, I have seen him going about the street picking their caps off.'

'But nothing of a serious nature?'

Thompson shook his head, 'Oh no, sir.'

Sampson then cut to the chase. 'I understand you don't generally believe what he does say. He is utterly unreliable, is he not?

'Yes,' said Thompson, and the coroner asked him to relate the events of the time when Wolstenholme came into the lodging house that morning after the murder of Elizabeth Peers. 'Well, sir, on the morning after the murder, Sunday morning that is, Wolstenholme came into the lodging house and hung up his muffler scarf to dry in the kitchen. A man named Wheeler then entered and told us that a little girl had been murdered off

Smithdown Road in an entry. A quarter of an hour later, Wolstenholme called me into the back-kitchen and suddenly told me that he had gone up the entry where the girl had been murdered and had seen a man in dark clothes coming out.'

'Did you pay any attention to his story?'

'No sir, I didn't,' said Thompson, 'He is so unreliable I scarcely take notice of what he says. He said he had been working, and then he said he hadn't.'

In the summing up, the coroner said 'A more dastardly act could never have been perpetrated than has been disclosed in this case, It was horrifying in its details, and it was intensified by the difficulties which surrounded the case by reason of the absolutely unreliable evidence of almost everyone connected with the case. From beginning to end the Peers family members seemed to be at sixes and sevens. They could not give any really connected account of their movements which would enable the police to obtain a starting point. The reason for this is pretty obvious when we consider the character of the individuals. The mother, when the crucial time came, could not even fix her memory and state anything at all that was reliable. Even when we appealed to her maternal instincts to help us discover the murderer of her child, she was unable to remember anything, owing to the drunken state in which she was at the time! The conditions under which these people live together are absolutely revolting!'

At this point, Mrs Peers burst into tears as she realised the coroner was referring to the drunkenness of her husband and the way she had sent little Lizzie out around midnight on that errand without even considering her safety. As soon as Mrs Peers brought her emotional outburst under control, the disgusted coroner continued with his summing up: 'The story of the Wolstenholme man was of a very singular nature and one which we are very scarcely able to credit. Still it was thought proper to lay the man's evidence before the jury, so that the public should know exactly what the police were endeavouring to do. Wolstenholme was proved to have told a lot of lies, and was a man who was in the habit of inventing stories with some semblance of truth in them. The police know the cause of the child's death, and how she had been foully murdered by violence of an indescribable nature, but they could not find out who had done it.'

And then the jury gave their verdict: wilful murder by persons unknown, and that the parents of the girl be severely censured for their drunkenness. The mother, in addition, for having sent the child out so late, and for her unnatural conduct after she found her daughter had not returned.

The parents of Elizabeth Peers were brought into the well of the court. All faces turned to them as the coroner addressed the mother. 'If you had been able to give a clear statement, the police might have found the murderer of your child. The difficulties of the case were enhanced by you not even being able to fix the time you sent the child out.'

Mrs Peers bowed her head and silently cried. Mr Sampson then turned his attention to Mr Peers.

'As to you, sir,' said the coroner, 'you should have asserted yourself and been master of your own household! Both of you should be ashamed of yourselves.'

'I knew I'd have the blame of it,' sobbed Mrs Peers.

That was in 1905. The killer of Elizabeth Peers was

never found, but just under three years later, another child was raped and murdered within a few miles of Cullen Street, and the police did not even consider the possibility that the Peers murderer had struck again. This next case was the abduction, rape and murder of a child three years younger than Lizzie Peers – Madge Kirby, and she is the subject of the next chapter.

The Madge Kirby Murder Mystery

Twilight gathered as the sad tale of the Madge Kirby murder began to unfold at 4.30 on the wintry afternoon of Monday, 6 January 1908. Seven-year-old Margaret T Kirby, known affectionately as Madge by her father, little brother and her friends, was playing in Kensington Gardens, just around the corner from her home at Number 55 Romilly Street, in the district of Kensington. Madge lived there with her three-year-old brother George, infant sister Emily, and her father, David Kirby, a 38-year-old journeyman plumber who was only just coming to terms with the death of his wife, Jane (née Coulter) who had died giving birth to their daughter Emily in September 1907. On this cold and dusky afternoon in January 1908, Madge had just left her school, St Michaels, and was playing with her young brother and seven-year-old Annie McGovern, Madge's best friend, who was also with her younger brother. All the children were by the reservoir, unaware that they were being watched by a homicidal paedophile.

A man dressed in black approached and then asked Madge Kirby if she would like to go for sweets with him. Madge was a beautiful young girl with long brown hair, large expressive blue eyes, and a fresh-faced complexion. That afternoon she wore a black shirt which was a little frayed at the sleeves (from the child's habit of rubbing her forearm against her school desk lid when she was bored), a blue pinafore, a black velvet bonnet with black strings, black stockings and laced boots. Madge stood out from the other children, so the sinister man in black had undoubtedly singled her out, and heaven knows how long he had kept watch on the little angel until he thought the time was right to strike.

Madge smiled and nodded at the stranger's suggestion, and the sinister man in black took her by the hand and walked away. Annie McGovern, Madge's little brother, and the other children, watched the man walk through the gate of Kensington Gardens with Madge and cross the high street. He led Madge down Cottenham Street, and that was the last time the children of Kensington Gardens saw their friend, and the last time little George Kirby would see his sister alive. George went home to tell his father what had happened, but Mr Kirby – who had left home that day at 6.30am for work, was working till late and didn't return home until 8.15pm.

The father went in search of his daughter but she was nowhere to be found, so he went to the police, and in doing so initiated a wide-scale hunt in which 5,000 empty houses were searched, as well as parks and lakes. There were door to door enquiries and mass house visits, but no trace of the missing girl could be found. David Kirby went home, sat down by the fire and gave in to grief. He had last seen his beloved daughter on Sunday night, just after he had put her to bed and kissed her goodnight. Neighbours and relatives rallied around the plumber, trying to reassure him that he would see her again. 'She'll turn up again soon, Davy,' said one of the sympatheic women of Romilly Street.

The police had taken descriptions of Madge's abductor from her playmates in Kensington Gardens that dusky afternoon, and Annie McGovern gave the best description of the miscreant. Annie said the man had been tall, dressed in black clothes with a white shirt, black tie, and a dark moustache. In a well-spoken voice, he had said to Madge, 'Will you come with me for some sweets?' Annie was sure she would recognise the man if she saw him again.

Eight-year-old Christopher Sheenan was another of the children who had witnessed the abduction, and he maintained that the stranger's words to Madge had been, 'Will you come with me, little girl, and I will buy you some sweets?' Christopher had watched the man take his friend away and hoped they would return with the sweets, but when they didn't come back, he simply went home for his usual bread and butter meal and thought no more of the incident.

Shop-boy Robert Woodside of 33 Smollett Street also came forward after the abduction to say how he had sighted Madge and her abductor at 5.30pm whilst taking an order to a house on Rupert Hill, Everton. Robert saw a man in a black suit who matched the description of the fiend given by the missing girl's friends, and he was leading a girl by the hand. As Robert got nearer to them, he recognised the girl as Madge Kirby, and she was crying. The man pulled her along quite violently when she cried, and the shop-boy shouted to her, 'Come on Madge!'

The man and Madge had passed Robert by now and Madge turned round as she heard him call her, and tried to get to him, but the stranger yanked the girl's arm and hurried up the Everton street, dragging his prey after him. At one point the abductor realised the shop-boy was following him, and he told Madge to stay by the railings on Rupert Hill. The abductor then ran after Robert Woodside, chasing him away then going back to grab Madge.

Jane Hughes also came forward after the disappearance of Madge Kirby to tell police that she believed she had served the abductor and Madge at the

Cocoa Rooms on Brownlow Hill between 6.30pm to 7pm on the day of the abduction. Jane said she had served bread, butter and tea to a man in dark clothes with a black moustache. He had a girl with him who answered the description of Madge Kirby, and Jane had served the child with a small cup of tea and an Eccles cake. The child's face was smeared with tears, and Jane even accurately described the black velvet bonnet she had worn at the time of her disappearance.

Almost eight months later, at 6.55am, on the morning of Tuesday, 11 August, Tom Moody, a woodcarver on his way to work, found a large sackcloth sugar bag on the pavement just outside Number 15 Great Newton Street, off Pembroke Place. The man became curious and cut open the sack, recoiling in horror when he saw the decomposed remains of a scantily-clad child. Whoever had put the child in that sack had bent the body in half in such a way, so that the back of the head was touching the back of the thighs. There had just been a heavy shower, yet the bag was dry, so it was deduced that it had only just been brought out of a nearby house before it was found on the rain-slicked pavement, and this was found to be the case, because police investigated a nearby derelict house at 15 Great Newton Street and discovered hair, shrivelled shreds of skin, and pieces of clothing in the cellar that matched the corpse's hair and clothing. Police suspected the worst, and David Kirby was shown the corpse. He immediately recognised the clothing. The body in the bag was all that remained of his little daughter Madge.

Mr Kirby never recovered from the murder of his beloved daughter, and later that day at his Kensington home on Romilly Street, he was heard to say, 'This will finish me,' and he collapsed on to his bed. The remains of Madge Kirby were lain to rest shortly afterwards at the Catholic Cemetery in Ford. Thousands of mourners from across Liverpool were moved to tears as they lined the route of the funeral cortege, and most of the shops in Kensington closed their shutters during the funeral procession. A touching tribute was a harp of flowers from little Annie McGovern, the child who had been Madge Kirby's best friend. Madge's father, David never rose again from his bed, and he died weeks later on 24 October from a broken heart.

The coroner, T E Sampson, recorded the cause of Madge's death as 'Vulgar violence followed by suffocation or strangulation, caused by some person or persons unknown – wilful murder.'

Weeks before David Kirby's death, on 13 August, a letter, written in the neat legible handwriting of a person of obvious education, was delivered to the police station on Prescot Street, sent from someone claiming to be the killer of Madge Kirby. It was addressed to Inspector Moore of the Liverpool Police, the man in charge of the Kirby case, and it said:

Dear Sir,
I should like to throw a little light on the murder of my victim, Madge Kirby. Some years ago I was a lodger at Number 15 Great Newton Street so that I know the house thoroughly and I am still in possession of a key to the front door, which I used in those days. On the night of January 6th at a quarter to nine I took the girl through the front door, and it was quite dark. We had been over to the 'World's Fair' before then ... That is the way I treated her, and then I did away with her. The

116

way I killed her you will no doubt find out today. At 5.35 on Tuesday morning last I entered the house once more with my key, not with the intention of moving the body for good, but with the intention of letting the world know what became of the child. If I had not been drinking I don't suppose I would have attempted the task. It may lead to my arrest, and only the drink have I to thank for it. I am now going to give you a real clue to work on. I am a regular at the public house mentioned. Since I have made this confession I will be obliged to say goodbye to [a person's name is given here]. I suppose they have been good friends to me ... I have given you a chance for your money now, so do your best, but I am sure your manhunt will be in vain.

The envelope containing this letter bore the address of the Prescot Street Bridewell, written in fine copperplate-style writing, and above it, four chilling words stated: 'From Maggie Kirby's murderer'.

Detectives working round the clock on the case made a painstaking search of 15 Great Newton Street, and, mindful of the letter-writer claim at being a former lodger at the house where Madge had probably died, they began to trace the former occupants of the Great Newton Street dwelling. In 1900, a man named George Webb had lived in Number 15, but had not taken in lodgers, and in 1901, a collector named Daniel Walsh had been the householder of Number 15. He could not be traced, but those who recalled him were certain he had not allowed lodgers in his home during his tenancy.

A year later, Number 15 came into the hands of a Jewish man, born in Liverpool in 1846, and he had possession of the house until 31 August 1903. His name was Nathaniel Schwersensky, and police traced the 62-year-old bill distributor and asked him if he had kept lodgers when he had lived at 15 Great Newton Street. Nathaniel said he had, and he recalled one lodger in particular, because he was a very odd man who acted strangely at times. His name was John Thompson. Mr Schwersensky recalled that Thompson was smartly-dressed with a dark moustache, and seemed to be a clerk. He had certainly struck him as an educated man, and few people seemed to know anything about him, but he was thought to have lodgings elsewhere, either in Everton Brow or St Anne Street.

If we cast our minds back to the unsolved 1905 murder of Elizabeth Peers at Edge Hill, we will recall that the surname Thompson is referred to twice. George Amos Wolstenholme claims he went to Widnes to see a man named Thompson to obtain work, and there is also a mention of a John Thompson who works as a kitchen man – in the lodging-house of Catherine James, at 41a St Anne Street. Is this a mere coincidence – or could the man who raped and murdered Elizabeth Peers and the beast who raped and murdered Madge Kirby be one and the same monster? Some thought there was a connection, and one letter-writer to the *Liverpool Echo* – a Mr W H Bradford, of 9 Sandstone Road, Stoneycroft, asked readers if there was a parallel between the murder of Kirby and Peers. Mr Bradford either had such a great interest in the Peers case that he had retained clippings of the newspaper coverage of the crime, or he had an extraordinary power of total recall, for within his letter to the *Liverpool Echo*, he mentioned, in great detail, the evidence of George Amos Wolstenholme at the inquest of the Cullen Street Crime, and of the man he said he had seen coming out of the entry, 'between 1.15am and 1.20am, on Sunday, 29 October 1905.' Bradford recalls that: 'the man looked alarmed and agitated, and he [Wolstenholme] said he looked thirty-five to forty years of age, about five feet ten inches tall, and had a dark moustache.'

Detectives quizzed the owners and workers of the World's Fair – a fairground also billed as Collins Fun City – that had been set up on waste-ground in nearby Gill Street, just off Great Newton Street, in January that year, in the hope that they might have seen the killer with Madge, for the author of the 'confessional' letter to the police had claimed he had been to the World's Fair with the abducted child before he raped and killed her. No one connected with the fairground could help the police. The fairground workers had seen thousands of people since and couldn't remember a man and a girl from such vague descriptions as those mentioned by the police.

Few clues were initially found in the cellar of 15 Great Newton Street. An ornamental fan was found, and the police thought this might have been given to Madge by the killer to amuse her until he was sure he would be able to assault her without her cries being heard in the street. Newspaper bills of the sort used by newsagents to advertise the papers of the local press, were found in the cellar and in the sack containing the body. These bills advertised the *Liverpool Express*, the *Liverpool Echo*, and a portion of a publication called the *Freethinker* was also found in the cellar. The bag the corpse was put in was a sugar sack of the type found in most grocery shops, but there were no marks upon it to tell the police which shop it had come from. A diligent detective finally noticed a clue which could have hanged Madge Kirby's murderer. On a door that the killer had to open with a jemmy to get into Number 15 Great Newton Street, he had left his fingerprints and even full handprints in the accumulated layer of dust on the door. These prints were photographed by the police. The door leading to the cellar itself had been nailed up, either by the Liverpool Corporation workers – as it was scheduled for demolition – or the killer after leaving the body inside, until he had returned to the house to remove it, perhaps in remorse, or, as the writer of the 11 August letter claimed – 'to let the world know' what had become of Madge Kirby.

Around this time, the public wanted to know why no reward was being offered by the police to catch Madge's killer. No reward was ever offered, and the police never specified why this was so.

During the inquest into the death of Madge Kirby, the coroner proceeded to read yet another letter, supposedly typed out by the self-accusing killer of the child. This one was dated London, 17 August 1908, and its contents painted a very sinister picture of the murderer: The letter read:

Dear Sir,

I told you I would give you a run for your money, and I mean to. Perhaps you didn't comprehend the delight that the chase gives me. You cannot understand any case that does not proceed from the lower orders. London is a large place with several millions of inhabitants; can you identify me? It is no good giving you a description of myself, because you would be sure to arrest some man without a single resemblance to me, and I don't want to get anyone into trouble. Moreover, you probably imagined that an epileptic always behaves in some odd manner; but let me tell you that with the exception of the times when the mania is on

me, I am a very normal person indeed. And if you could see me now, sitting in a merchant's office, typing this to you, you would be the last to think I could be the man you are looking for. If the man who has given me the use of his machine for half an hour could be told that I did to death that Kirby child, his incredulity would be amusing in the extreme. On the whole, I would not advise you to send to London to find me, as my stay in the metropolis is of a rather uncertain duration. If you have any friends there whom you are wanting to visit, why not come yourself? You could get all your expenses paid, and would be regarded as a zealous officer. Liverpool could well spare your services for a few days, and you would get a pleasant holiday, for which you might thank me. If you come down, and I am still here, I shall endeavour to see you under some pretext or another. In that case I will write again to let you know at what places I was near you. You know, that it is no good searching the house in Great Newton Street, simply because I don't happen to be there at present. I throw out this advice to you for what it is worth, as it may save you a little time and trouble, and if you come to London you can go to the Exhibition. It is quite worth seeing. I went there myself last Saturday and found one could see very little in one visit.
Yours as before,
LITTLE KIRBY'S KILLER

Other letters came from London, seemingly written by the same correspondent as the aforementioned missive, and these were signed 'The King of Darkness'.

Known and suspected child-molesters were quickly arrested by the police after discovery of the body on

121

Great Newton Street. One of these suspected paedophiles was a man named John Bishop, who was arrested and detained at the Cheapside bridewell for 24 hours after intensive questioning by detectives. Several women and a man had claimed to have seen Bishop in the company of a girl who looked like Madge Kirby just after the latter had been abducted, but Bishop was able to convince the police that these people had been mistaken, and was subsequently released.

Another suspect who was quizzed over the Kirby murder was Alfred George Noakes. Noakes was arrested in the following year, in the summer of 1909, after several people swore they had seen him with a girl dressed exactly like Madge on that fateful January day when the child was abducted. The stipendiary magistrate said there was not a shred of evidence to support Noakes being the murderer, and the prisoner was released, but had to move away from the city afterwards because of the infamy attached to the accusations levied against him.

The police were as desperate as the man and woman in the street to catch Madge Kirby's killer, so they decided to try bloodhounds. An amazing bloodhound named Czar, owned by a dog handler named Pakenham (who, as black coincidence would have it, lived in the street next to murder victim Elizabeth Peers), was deployed, along with another, less gifted bloodhound, which was used as a decoy to attract the enormous crowds that had been congregating outside Prescot Street Police Station. The crowd of 2,000 saw the bogus bloodhound rush out of the station, and followed it in droves. Many of the spectators were on bicycles, some had packed sandwiches and other refreshments, ready for the long trek. There were women pushing prams, an old army veteran on a horse, and even two people being pushed in wheelchairs as the decoy bloodhound set off towards Great Newton Street.

Just after midnight, as soon as the crowds had dispersed, Czar – who had been given the scent of Madge Kirby's clothes – came sniffing his way out the police station and immediately took the police on a curious journey. He went to the Botanic Gardens on Edge Lane and led the constables around the park. The dog then left the park and kept circling a patch of waste ground on the eastern extremities of Edge Lane. From there the dog led them to Tunnel Road, on the border of Edge Hill and Wavertree, where he went wild. Czar dragged the policeman into Edge Hill Railway Station, where he went straight for a the city-centre-bound platform. He stood stock still, then sniffed the air in a convulsed state. He then turned his head left, and looked down the railway tunnel. That tunnel led to Lime Street Station.

The police bundled the bloodhound into a taxicab which took them to Lime Street Station. When the bloodhound arrived at the station he ran straight to Platform 1 and barked towards the tunnel. The trains from that platform went to Birmingham. The dog's owner was of the opinion that the child murderer had left Liverpool for the Midlands at that platform the night before.

Once again, the hunt for Madge Kirby's killer had come to a dead end. Several members of the public meanwhile, had some strange tales to tell about a sinister-looking man they had seen prowling about in the alleyways behind Great Newton Street around the time the body was found there in the sack. This man had been dressed in women's clothing. The man was said to have been seen climbing over the backyard of the house where the body had been stored. Police said that the wall showed signs of having been climbed over. Some claimed the strange cross-dresser had been responsible for several assaults on children off Smithdown Road earlier in the year. Police now strongly suspected that the strange man Thompson, first named by Nathaniel Schwersensky, had been the murderer of Madge Kirby, but he was never traced.

Later in the year, police in Dewsbury received another letter from a man claiming he was Madge's killer. He warned that he was staying in the area for one week, then he would kill. Thankfully there were no further child-killings, and the letter was, in all probability, a sick hoax. The murderer of Madge Kirby, then, was never brought to justice. Ballads were sung about the child, and she entered into the dark pantheon of Liverpool folklore.

Madge's younger brother George died in 1960 at 58 Clapham Road, Anfield. Sadly, in the year after Madge's murder, the youngest member of the family, Emily Kirby, died from a fever, aged 19 months, after she had been taken to a doctor's surgery at 93 Shaw Street.

A woman I talked to named Joan once told me how, many years ago in the 1950s, when she was a child, she had been playing hide and seek in Ford Cemetery with her friends, and had hidden behind a gravestone close to the Kirby family grave. Upon the grave there was a beautiful glass-domed ornament containing flowers and a plaster of Paris statue of the Sacred Heart with a quotation from the New Testament upon a satin scroll. An old man with a white beard came along, unaware that he was being watched – and started to swear and spit at the Kirby grave, then smashed the glass-domed tribute to smithereens with his walking stick. Joan gasped in horror at this act of desecration, and got up to run off from behind the gravestone. The man shouted something after her, and Joan was in tears by the time she left the cemetery.

Was that old man just demented, or is it possible that he was the murderer of Madge Kirby? We'll probably never know. One thing is sure though, whoever he was, he has long taken his dreadful secret with him to the grave, and hopefully he has met his maker and been dispatched to a very warm place ...

THE MURDER OF NELLIE CLARKE

Nellie Clarke was a highly-strung 11-year-old with a terrible fear of darkness, and she had a particular phobia about unlit alleyways. She lived at 16 Byrne Avenue, Rock Ferry with her 13-year-old brother John, her mother, Sarah Good and stepfather, Peter Carr. Nellie's father, John Wallace Clarke had been killed in France during the First World War. Saturday, 10 January 1925 was quite an eventful day for little Nellie. She attended a party the Lord Mayor had given for 600 orphans of soldiers, and she and her older brother John came home, each with a gift from the Mayor himself. Nellie had received a doll she had christened Betty and John had been given a gleaming chrome harmonica.

Nellie was playing with her doll at 7.45pm that cold January Saturday evening, when her mother asked her to run an errand to the baker's shop. Nellie set off and her mother told John to go after his sister and tell her to fetch some cakes back as well, and this he did. Around 8pm John and Nellie came home together laughing, each unaware that they would never see one another again.

Nellie was sent out yet again at around 8.10pm – to a shop at 201 Old Chester Road – and her brother John asked his mother if he could go with her. 'No, you'd better stay in,' said Mrs Clarke sternly, 'when you two go out together there's no knowing when you'll return.'

Sporting a red tam o'shanter, and a red and white striped blouse frock under a brown coat, Nellie looked smart as usual when she called at the shop on Old Chester Road, but the girl never returned home, and her parents and brother became concerned for her safety.

Mrs Good and her son went in search of Nellie without success, yet there were several sightings of the girl that Saturday evening. Her classmate Lillian Smith saw Nellie going towards New Chester Road on her own, walking apart from a group of children in front of her. That was around 8pm, but Lillian couldn't be certain what time it was. Around 9.50pm, a Mrs Green of Spenser Avenue heard a loud bang at her front door, followed by a rattle of her letter-box. Then came a shriek – then nothing. Mrs Green ran to the door but there was nobody there and the avenue was eerily silent. The woman's young son, Robert, had also heard the spine-chilling scream, but he had heard more than his mother, for Robert had been startled by a girl's frantic voice crying out: 'Father Christmas is after me! Let me in!'

The search for Nellie Clarke went on into the early hours of a wintry Sunday morning, and at 8.25am, Martin Doran of 1 Highfield Grove, discovered the body of a girl propped against a telegraph pole in the entry outside his backyard. It was the body of Nellie Clarke. She had been raped and strangled to death, and her body had been left in a passageway she had hurried past many times because of her fear of dark entries. There was a dark and discoloured oval mark under her right ear, as well as various bruises on the left side of the throat, made by the fingers of the killer.

Mr Doran, the painter and decorator who found the body outside his backyard, had slept in his room overlooking the scene, yet he had heard nothing during the night, and stranger still, his dogs had not even barked in the yard that night, and those dogs barked at anyone who came down the alleyway. The manager of Milne's Butchers Shop said he saw Nellie walking towards

Bedford Street, Rock Ferry, with a tall smartly-dressed man, and the description matched the one given by a taxi-driver who picked up a fare at 10pm on the night of the murder. The man, who had appeared to be agitated, had said to the cabby: 'Take me to St Paul's Road ... quickly!' The cab-driver obeyed and later that night was having a drink in the nearby Royal Standard Hotel, when in walked the suspicious man he'd picked up earlier. The man had a drink then left. He was in his early 40s, about five feet ten, smartly attired, slender, and dark-haired. He was never seen again in the area.

Mediums were consulted, but their 'information' was useless. A bloodhound was used in the hunt for Nellie's killer, and after sniffing the dead girl's clothes, it bolted off to waste ground close to the place where the child's body had been found and started to scratch away the soil. It uncovered a rosary Nellie had lost weeks before her death. The dog then bounded down Rock Lane West and proceeded to an alleyway near some allotments behind Rock Ferry Congregational Church. When the bloodhound reached a corrugated iron sheet shed, used as a tools store, it stopped dead, but the police took this lead no further.

An anonymous letter, written on distinctive pink notepaper, was sent to the police from one half of a courting couple who had been standing in the shadows of the entry off Spenser Avenue, where Nellie's body was dumped. The author of the letter, believed to have been a woman, said she and her beau had seen an agile man carrying a child in his arms as he passed by, but neither of them had been aware the girl was dead at that time, so had thought no more of it. The letter bore a Manchester postmark. On 18 January that year, eight days after the

Nellie Clarke murder, 13-year-old Lower Bebington schoolgirl, Edith Rose Colley, went missing. Everyone thought she had been murdered by the same monster who had killed Nellie, but two days later she turned up alive and well; she'd been wandering about in Chester. Edith had written a goodbye note to her father before the disappearance on pink writing paper, yet her father was baffled at this, because he kept no pink stationery in his home. The paper was of the same type the anonymous letter from Manchester had been written on, but the police apparently didn't notice this.

Nellie Clarke's killer was never brought to secular justice – but I suspect his maker has long since dealt with him. Many times over the years, the solid-looking ghost of Nellie Clarke has been seen leaning against the telegraph pole where her killer left her after he'd molested and choked her. Some say her tragic ghost occasionally roams the streets of Rock Ferry where she used to play, and there have been alleged sightings of the girl walking forlornly along Byrne Avenue, where she once lived.

THE MAN IN THE IRON TUBE

While clearing up rubble from the aftermath of a German air raid on Liverpool in 1943, a group of American soldiers probably assumed that the long black metal tube protruding from the bottom of the bomb crater near Great Homer Street was a piece of shattered pipe. The GIs tried to dislodge the piece of 'piping' with a mechanical digger, but it wouldn't budge. In the summer of that year a second attempt was made to remove the obstruction with a more powerful mechanical digger, and this time the tubular piece of scrap was successfully uprooted.

As the dust settled, it became apparent that the metallic tube was no ordinary pipe, but a riveted sheet-iron cylinder six feet nine inches in length and 18 inches in diameter. However, the sealed cylinder aroused no more than a passing interest amongst the soldiers, who had more pressing matters to attend to, and so the tube was left among the debris of the blitzed site. And there it lay forgotten until Friday, 13 July 1945, when a nine-year-old boy playing on the bombed wasteland came across the unidentified relic while playing hide-and-seek with his friends.

Little Tommy Lawless was hiding behind the tube when he noticed a boot poking out from a hole in one end. Tommy, who had never owned a pair of boots in his life, was delighted at his find, thinking that his barefoot days were over at last. He gently pulled the boot free – and saw to his horror that it had come off the foot of a skeleton. Terrified, Tommy fled from his startled playmates, and did not stop running until he saw PC Robert Baillie walking his beat in Great Homer Street.

Breathlessly the youngster told the policeman what he had found, and in so doing launched the inquiry into the baffling case of the Man in the Iron Tube.

Shortly after 1pm that day the cylinder and its gruesome contents were taken to the city morgue. After a detailed description of the strange artefact had been recorded, an engineer was called in to open the cylinder with an oxy-acetylene blowtorch. When the smoking tube was finally cut open, Dr Charles Harrison and the engineer looked at its skeletal occupant in astonishment. To Harrison, senior lecturer in pathology at Liverpool University, it was evident that he was about to have the unusual task of performing a post-mortem on a body that must date back to the age of Queen Victoria.

The skeleton was resplendent in a morning coat, striped narrow trousers and the fine pair of elastic-sided boots that had caught the eye of little Tommy Lawless. The position of the cadaver was strange: it lay lengthwise along the tube on a bed of sacking with its skull (which still had hair attached to it) resting on a pillow that consisted of a brick wrapped in a sack, suggesting that the man in the tube had been sleeping when he died.

Doctor Harrison's examination revealed that the body was that of a six-foot-tall middle-aged male. On the finger bone of one hand, the corpse wore a gold signet ring bearing a green stone flecked with red. But that was all the doctor was able to say about the mysterious corpse. He could not explain how the man in the tube had met his death.

The police called in Dr J B Firth, a highly respected forensic expert from Preston, whose examination produced some intriguing results. Among the remains he discovered seven keys, and also two diaries: one book contained entries for July 1884 and the other for June of that year. From a pocket in the dead man's morning coat, Firth extracted a bundle of papers that were encapsulated in a revolting wax-like substance, the residue of the body's decomposed tissue. Firth skilfully applied various organic solvents to the waxen lump and with great perseverance finally managed to extricate 13 separate documents. Most of the documents referred to a certain T C Williams & Co. of Leeds Street, Liverpool. A postcard among the recovered papers was also addressed to T C Williams.

Now that the police had a name to work with, their investigation could begin in earnest. Detective Inspector John Morris delved into the city's archives and scoured the electoral registers of the 1880s. In a business register for 1883 he came across a firm trading under the name of T C Williams & Co. at 18 to 20 Leeds Street. The firm was described in the yellowed text of the old register as 'Oil Merchants, Paint & Varnish Manufacturers'. Morris established that the head of the firm was a Mr Thomas Cregeen Williams, who lived at 29 Clifton Road, Anfield. Moreover, the inspector discovered that in the following year the financial affairs of the plant works were for some reason being investigated by a firm of accountants. What became of the company after that is a mystery, for there is no further reference to the business in any of the Liverpool trade directories after 1884.

Inspector Morris searched the local registers for some record of the death of Thomas Cregeen Williams, but could find none. Morris hypothesised that Mr Williams had hidden himself from his creditors by crawling into the metal tube and had died from accidental asphyxiation. But it is an unsatisfactory theory. In the

1880s it was more usual for debtors simply to board a ship and work their passage abroad when their creditors got too threatening. Thomas Cregeen Williams is listed in a column detailing liquidations in the *Liverpool Mercury* for 8 September 1883, and his residential addresses are given as 29 Cambridge Road, Seaforth, and Woodville House, Abbotsford Road, Blundellsands – where he was staying that month. The meeting with his creditors took place, according to this column, at the offices of Mr W H Harris, 4 Harrington Street, Liverpool.

Tantalisingly, Firth's examination of the Man in the Iron Tube reached a dead end. The forensic expert analysed the clothes and bones of the corpse for traces of poison but could find none. So what are we to make of the unknown man? How did he come to die in his cylindrical coffin? Was he murdered? Or was he a murderer hiding from justice? The questions remain unanswered.

THE OLD CURIOSITY SHOP MURDER

In most people's minds the Liverpool district of Aintree is usually associated with its racecourse, where the world-famous Grand National is run each year, but early in 1953, Aintree featured in the newspaper headlines because a timid old man was brutally murdered within its vicinity.

Just a mile from Aintree racecourse, there stands a grand Victorian detached house, 98 Warbreck Moor. It was once the home of Hugh George Walker, a retired and increasingly reclusive 82-year-old tailor who liked to hoard antiques and bric-a-brac in the shop he ran on the ground floor of his house. This magpie's nest was known to the locals as the 'Old Curiosity Shop', and at 2.30pm on Friday, 9 January 1953, 20-year-old John Todd called at Walker's premises. Todd, a pale-faced man with a prominent pointed nose and a distinctive wart at the side of his left eye, loved to tinker about with anything mechanical, and broken watches and clocks were his speciality.

Old Mr Walker's sister, Mary, who lived in the Tuebrook district of Liverpool, immediately thought there was something sinister about the pallid young man. As Todd entered the shop one day, she noticed a knife dangling in a sheath attached to his waistband. Mr Walker, on the other hand, apparently liked Todd, and let him work unsupervised among his stock upstairs, telling his suspicious sister that Todd was merely working on a troublesome grandfather clock.

Mary Walker saw Todd again on Monday, 12 January. He was still attempting to fix the grandfather clock, and now seemed very familiar with her brother, calling him 'Pop' and joking with him.

On the afternoon of 13 January two schoolboys – Ronald Cole and Allan Lake – called at Walker's shop, hoping to purchase valves for a radio set, but John Todd answered the door and told them to come back the next day.

On the following day at around 2.15pm, John Todd picked up the axe that Mr Walker used to break up large lumps of coal for his fire, and brought it down on the head of the 82-year-old man a total of 32 times. After a couple of blows, Mr Walker's legs gave way and he collapsed on to the vestibule floor at the foot of the staircase. As Walker lay there spreadeagled, the savage John Todd continued to whack the old man's head. Pieces of skull flew across the hallway during the sickening attack, and bloody brain-tissue spattered the walls – and Todd's fawn-coloured raincoat. Fifteen seconds into the attack, the axe's shaft broke, preventing the clock-mender from continuing his merciless slaughter.

John Todd surveyed what he had done. The well-liked old introvert lay fatally stricken in an ever-widening pool of blood. The silver pocket-watch, an item of enormous sentimental value to its owner, was snatched from Walker's waistcoat. Todd walked upstairs to the scullery in a daze and dropped the blood-coated axehead into an enamel bowl of water. He discarded the stained raincoat, then returned to the hallway and tramped through the pool of lukewarm blood on his way to the front door of Number 98, his crepe soles squelching as he went. Todd left the shop with the silver pocket-watch he had murdered for.

Out in the street Mr Walker's two dogs – an old Scottish terrier and a young mongrel – started to whine, as if they had some sense of their owner's violent demise. They ran to the door of the shop and began to bark, but passers-by did not realise there was anything sinister about the behaviour of the distressed animals.

At 7.40pm John Todd visited his 22-year-old girlfriend at her home, Number 2 Park Grove in Bootle. Raven-haired Iris Tucker had met John 18 months earlier while working as an usherette at the Bedford Cinema in the Walton district of Liverpool, and it had been a case of love at first sight. Since that night when their eyes met, Todd had visited his sweetheart every evening without fail, although Iris's father wasn't keen on her boyfriend, and rarely spoke to him.

Iris noticed on this occasion that Todd was not wearing his sheath knife, and asked him what had become of it.

'I won't be wearing it any more, love,' was Todd's enigmatic reply.

Back at Warbreck Moore, Mr Walker's dogs were still barking, and they continued to bay into the night. The commotion woke Mrs Lawson, a neighbour of the murdered man, and she went to the shop and rang the bell. Lawson knew how long it usually took for the decrepit shop-owner to answer the door, so she waited – and waited. Twenty minutes later, Mrs Lawson stopped hammering on the door and ringing the bell and decided to return home. She surmised that Mr Walker had gone to visit his sister.

Almost 24 hours later, the exhausted dogs were still whining at the door of their dead master's shop. Then the mongrel suddenly parted company with the Scottish terrier and ran off to the next street. It went to the door of Mrs Marion Owen, a woman who often treated Walker's

136

dogs to the occasional bone. The little mongrel barked at Mrs Owen's front door at 21 Hall Lane, and when she answered and saw the fretful animal, she knew something was wrong. After getting no answer at the Curiosity Shop, Mrs Owen phoned the police and told them that she had reason to believe that something dreadful had happened to old Mr Walker.

Sergeant Hosker of Rice Lane Police Station quickly responded to the call. He hammered on the door of Number 98, and after receiving no reply, charged at the door and forced it open. Hosker took a small torch from his pocket and shone it into the dark hallway. The disc of light flitted about the walls of the corridor, then dropped down to stop on the body of Mr Walker. The sergeant located the light-switch, flicked it, and a dim low-wattage light-bulb revealed the heinous scene – but the sergeant was unaware of the faint trail of bloody footprints that had been left by John Todd's crepe soles. Hosker shook his head as he surveyed the slivers of skull scattered about the hallway. The policeman had seen some stomach-churning sights in his time, but he had never seen a murder victim of Mr Walker's advanced age, and this really sickened the sergeant.

Fearful of disturbing evidence, Hosker retreated from the murder house and looked sympathetically at Mr Walker's loyal dogs as they tilted their heads quizzically and looked upon their dead owner. Sergeant Hosker went to his car to radio the news of the gruesome discovery, and in doing so launched a major murder hunt. Chief superintendent Herbert Balmer headed the inquiry and his first action was to call for the services of the brilliant Home Office pathologist Dr Arthur St Hill of Huyton. Hill promptly arrived at the murder scene and had the body of Mr Walker taken to the City Mortuary, where a thorough post-mortem was carried out. Dr St Hill told Balmer of the 32 lacerations on the deceased man's skull and face. The skull and left cheekbones had been smashed during the prolonged and vicious attack, and the pathologist had managed to fit some of the bone fragments back together like some grotesque jigsaw puzzle.

Balmer immediately arranged for the area surrounding the 'Old Curiosity Shop' to be cordoned off, and a house-to-house inquiry disrupted the sleep of almost a hundred residents in the streets around Warbreck Moor.

Later, around 6am, Dr J B Firth and a group of other forensic experts invaded Walker's shop. They examined the crimson streaks on the hallway walls and they also came to notice the faint outline of the bloody footprints. The forensic team employed the recently discovered technique of photographing the footprints in special lights that had been designed to enhance faint outlines by illuminating them from an oblique angle. In the developed photographs the prints of John Todd's crepe soles showed up with pristine clarity.

The broken axe handle lying near the body was examined and found to fit exactly with the wooden piece of broken shaft still connected to the axehead in the bowl of water upstairs. What was obviously the murder weapon was taken away for analysis.

Two days later Balmer attended a press conference and revealed that the police were seeking a man of about 30 who mended clocks and watches for a living. Balmer gave the description of this sought-after individual: 'He has a thin pale face, a long pointed nose, and a distinctive whitish wart at the side of his left eye. He is about five feet eight inches tall, and was last seen wearing a fawn-coloured gabardine raincoat.'

Balmer and his detectives had heard a variety of descriptions of Todd during their enquiries, but the descriptions given by Mary Walker and the two schoolboys, Lake and Cole, who had visited the shop on the eve of the murder, had been invaluable.

Almost a week after the brutal murder, Todd's girlfriend, Iris Tucker, picked up the morning paper and read of the Aintree killing, which the press were calling 'The Old Curiosity Shop Murder'. She sipped a cup of tea as she perused the newspaper's account of the terrible deed and was quite sickened by the article. She wondered how anybody could stoop to killing a defenceless old man in such a heinous, brutal way. Iris's heart then skipped a beat when she read the description of the wanted man. In total disbelief she read and re-read of the watch-mender with the wart at the side of his left eye. Iris shared her fears with her father, who told her that they had no choice but to inform the police. He grabbed his coat and walked to the nearest telephone box to call Bootle Police Station. Detective Chief Inspector Morris, Detective Sergeant Metcalfe and Detective Constable Hall arrived at 2 Park Grove and quizzed Iris Tucker. She told them what they wanted to know, and within 15 minutes they were knocking on the door of a house in Roxburgh Street, Walton, where John Todd lived with his mother. Todd was taken to Rice Lane Police Station and grilled for almost five hours before being charged with the murder of Mr Walker.

'No,' was Todd's reaction to the charge, his voice barely audible.

'What?' Chief Inspector Morris impatiently queried the young man's faint utterance.

'Only I know I didn't murder him.' Todd replied.

On the following day, as Hugh George Walker was being buried in Everton Cemetery, John Lawrence Todd found himself in court before Liverpool stipendiary magistrate Arthur McFarlane, represented by Harry Livermore, and the prosecuting solicitor was Mr A E West. West told the court of Todd's far-fetched version of the events that occurred in the shop on the day of the murder. In his signed statement he said:

> As I was leaving on the Wednesday, the old man tripped and fell against me. His nose hit my shoulder and started bleeding. His nose rubbed down the front of my raincoat as I tried to get my hands under his arms to try to stop him falling down, but I did not succeed. I then helped him up to see what had caused him to trip. I saw a type of adze or axe on the floor. I picked up the head, as the handle was broken, took the head up to the kitchenette and put it in the bottom shelf of the food cabinet.

Despite his denials, things were looking very grim for the accused, and at the end of the three-day hearing, Todd was committed for trial at Liverpool Assizes at St George's Hall on 8 April 1953.

At the start of the trial, Todd pleaded not guilty to the charge of murder. Prosecuting counsel Edward Wooll QC informed the jury – which consisted of ten men and two women – of the claims made in Todd's statement, then called for Dr J B Firth, the forensic expert, to provide evidence. Firth told the court of the blood found inside the trouser pocket and jacket cuff of Todd's blue suit. Mr Walker's blood group was O. The blood on Todd's suit was also Group O. This same type of blood was detected on Todd's fawn raincoat – found at the scene of the crime. Blood of Group O was also found on the uppers of Todd's pair of brown crepe-soled shoes, although Firth stated that he had found no blood on the shoes.

Dr Arthur St Hill was called to give evidence, and he presented the court with the findings of the post-mortem carried out on the murdered man. Dr St Hill also gave details of the bloody footprints discovered in the hallway of Mr Walker's shop, and he calmly gave a blow-by-blow account of a grisly experiment he had conducted during the course of his investigations. Several members of the jury looked queasy as Dr St Hill described how he had got a laboratory worker at the Forensic Unit at Preston to stand in a tray of human blood, wearing crepe soles to soak up the blood. Dr St Hill then asked the lab worker to walk specific distances on the pavement outside the building in order to discover how long it would take for the blood to be walked off the soles. The macabre experiment was carried out on a rainy day, and Dr St Hill found, to his surprise, that there was no detectable blood on the crepe soles after the lab worker had walked just 400 yards. Therefore the absence of blood on Todd's crepe shoes was no indication of his innocence.

Mr Wooll later called Todd's girlfriend to the witness box. Iris told the court how she had come to meet John and how long she had known him. She was shown a pair of brown crepe-soled shoes, a fawn raincoat, and a blue suit. Wooll asked Iris Tucker if she had seen these items of clothing before, and she confirmed that they had been worn by Todd on the day of the murder. Iris also mentioned something of obvious significance during one of her statements: that her boyfriend had mentioned losing his raincoat on the day of the murder. He said he'd mislaid it as he was looking for work at Sandon Dock. Iris Tucker also recalled how, hours after the murder in Aintree, Todd had called at her house wearing an unfamiliar blue suit, unlike the blue suit he usually wore.

Mary Walker, the murdered man's sister, was called to the witness box next, and she told the court about Todd's visits to the shop to fix the grandfather clock, and what she said was corroborated by Ronald Cole and Allan Lake – the schoolchildren who had spoken to Todd after calling at the shop on the day before the murder.

David Harrison, a jeweller who had repaired Mr Walker's watch in September 1951, was given the watch found in the possession of John Todd, and claimed it was Mr Walker's old silver pocket-watch, without a shadow of a doubt. 'Are you sure that is the watch you repaired in 1951?'

'I am absolutely certain it is,' Harrison replied.

Miss Rose Heilbron QC had the daunting task of presenting a realistic defence. She rehashed the dubious tale about Mr Walker falling against Todd with a bleeding nose, but the story seemed more contrived each time the court heard it. Miss Heilbron ended her examination by putting a question to Todd. She asked him if he had killed Mr Walker, and in an unusually raised voice Todd replied: 'I did not kill Mr Walker!'

At this point Mr Justice Cassels decreed, 'I think this is a convenient moment to adjourn until tomorrow.'

Mr Wooll cross-examined John Todd on the following day, and got him to admit that his raincoat had not been misplaced at Sandon Dock at all; but Todd then went on to say that, although he had lied about the raincoat, the silver watch which jeweller David Harrison had identified as Mr Walker's, was in fact his own. Todd was asked to elaborate and said he had received the watch from a mysterious man named John Arthur at the Bedford Cinema some 18 months ago.

Mr Wooll took hold of a graphic black and white photograph showing the butchered corpse of Hugh George Walker lying in the hallway, and held it up to Todd. As the young man blinked and looked away from the photograph, Wooll said, 'When the old man fell after bruising his nose, did he fall like that?'

'No,' Todd said, in a subdued and choked-up voice.

'How did the bloodstains get on your raincoat?' Wooll asked.

'He just ... he just bled on me,' was Todd's hollow explanation.

'So I take it that this gory mess is subsequent to your leaving?' said Wooll, pointing to the stark, disturbing photograph.

'Yes,' Todd looked down to his fidgeting hands.

The young man then stepped down from the witness box after giving evidence for a duration of two hours and 15 minutes.

During the final address to the jury, Wooll recounted the significance of the silver watch and the fawn raincoat. In turn, Miss Heilbron gave her summary of Todd's cobweb-thin defence, end by saying, 'Todd comes to you not as a man of petty convictions or grave convictions against him, but as a man of sterling character, and if ever a character could be weighed in the balance, I am sure you will take that into account. Todd is a very ordinary young man living with his mother.'

And in the summing-up to the jury Mr Justice Cassels said, 'No man is to be convicted on a charge such as this merely because he told lies, but you are not to leave out of your consideration the reflection as to why he told lies. If you are satisfied that this was the hand that struck those thirty-two savage blows on that defenceless old man's head, and thus battered the life out of him, you will return a verdict of guilty.'

The jury returned a verdict of guilty after one hour of deliberation. As the black cap was placed on the head of Mr Justice Cassels, John Todd's face remained expressionless. Cassels gazed at Todd and informed him: 'The sentence upon you is that you be taken from this place to a lawful prison, and from thence to a place of execution, there to suffer death by hanging, and that your body be buried within the precincts of the prison in which you were last confined before your execution, and may the Lord have mercy on your soul.'

Defence counsel Harry Livermore lost no time in lodging an appeal, and Miss Heilbron also appealed against Todd's conviction at the Court of Criminal Appeal. But Mr Justice Croom-Johnson dismissed the case, saying there was 'nothing in it'.

Livermore sent a letter to David Maxwell Fyfe, the Home Secretary, urgently requesting a medical enquiry into John Todd's sanity. 'I am unable to comply with the request,' was Fyfe's written reply.

And so executioner Albert Pierrepoint and his assistant John Broadbent were summoned to Walton Prison to dispatch John Todd. The young man who robbed the life of a frail old man was hanged on the Tuesday morning of 19 May 1953.

A week after the execution, the RSPCA found a new

home for Mr Walker's pets – the faithful dogs that had alerted the residents of Warbreck Moor to the terrible murder of their master.

THE HANGING BOY MYSTERY

Around 10 o'clock on the Saturday night of 2 February 1946, 14-year-old Ernie Johnson from Number 13 Watford Road in Anfield, decided to call upon his cousin Charles Greeney, the 11-year-old son of Maureen, a money lender, and Charles, a plasterer. When Ernie arrived at Number 62 Edge Lane, he found the front door open, the radiogramme still playing, and all the lights on in the large house, which had 11 rooms. The place had been ransacked and it was obvious there had been a break-in.

When Ernie looked in the kitchenette, he found his cousin Charlie Greeney hanging by his neck from the clothes rack. He seemed to be dead. Ernie ran out the house and informed the neighbours next door about the murder. He then rushed just 200 yards to a hotel where the dead boy's parents were having their usual Saturday evening drink. The parents returned to the house and the father took Charlie down from the rack and tried to give him a drink of water in a vain effort to resuscitate him, but it was no use, the boy was dead.

The value of property that had been taken from the house was valued at £600. Expensive clocks, a huge fawn Wilton carpet, brand new suits, fur coats and various other expensive items had been stolen, but the safe in the office where Mrs Greeney carried out her money-lending business was untouched. The family's seven-month-old bull terrier pup was in the yard outside the kitchen where the hanging had taken place, and although the pup barked whenever strangers called, the neighbours all agreed that it had not made a sound that night.

The only clue to the burglary and murder was an

Albion van that had been seen parked on Dorothy Street, just around the corner from the house. Chief Superintendent Fothergill wondered if the burglars had been recognised by Charlie, and if they had therefore killed him to ensure he remained silent. Or, as another detective suggested, was it possible that the burglars had broken into the house and found the boy hanging as they were ransacking the place?

Five men were soon arrested for the burglary and four of them were also held on suspicion of murder. A sixth man was arrested in Gibraltar. All four swore they had not killed Charlie Greeney. Two of the men said that when they broke into the house, they came across Charlie standing on a chair in front of a fireplace with his back towards them. He was not moving, and they at first assumed he was deaf, so they proceeded to burgle the other rooms.

The inquest proved that Charlie could not have hanged himself and hoisted his own body up on to the clothes rack, but frustratingly, the investigation ended up coming to a tantalising halt. The four accused men were found not guilty of murder. The judge summed up the strange case by saying, 'Although we are not certain that it was an accident, we are not certain that it was not.'

The hanging of Charles Greeney is therefore still an unsolved mystery today.

THE DAVID ECCLES MURDER

Ghosts – if you choose to believe in them – sometimes have an uncanny knack of teaching you all about the dark side of local history.

In the late 1990s, the glowing spectre of a boy of about eight or nine years of age was seen in the basement of the central post office on Liverpool's Victoria Street (now the site of the Met Quarter). A woman working in the building saw the apparition close up and said there was blood coming from the child's ears, and he was also sobbing. A so-called medium was called in and claimed the boy had died in the Blitz. The clairvoyant also said he sensed that the spectral boy's name was John. I asked the medium if he could provide a surname, which would be of enormous help in identifying the boy when I consulted various archives and records. He grimaced and said he couldn't get the ghost's second name.

I'm suspicious about self-proclaimed mediums who can only get a first name of a spirit and not the surname; surely if a first name comes through, it doesn't take much more effort to get the surname? I knew of a 60-year-old woman named Barbara who was genuinely psychic, and brought her to the haunted basement. Immediately she told me the boy's name wasn't John at all, but David, and she said he spoke with a Lancashire accent. He had not died in the Blitz as the other 'medium' had claimed, but had been murdered well before the Second World War, back in Victorian times. 'He's got no clothes,' Barbara told me, with tears in her eyes. Thanks to this and other information supplied by Barbara, I pieced together the following tragic tale.

On Sunday, 6 September 1891, Mary O'Brien, the mother of Robert Shearon, her eight-year-old 'illegitimate' problem child, decided that the only way she could stop the wayward boy from sneaking out of his Liverpool home at night was to deprive him of his clothes. Robert soon found a way round this predicament by cutting three holes in a sack for his arms and head, and he sneaked out of the house after dark, in search of his older friend, nine-year-old Sam Crawford, who formulated a wicked plan to obtain clothes for his associate.

In Great Charlotte Street on the following day at 2pm, Robert met a boy his own age named David Eccles. David, the son of a foundry worker, was smartly dressed in fine clothes, and wore a cap and a pair of new well-polished boots. Like Robert and Sam, he was also playing truant that afternoon. Robert introduced his new acquaintance to Sam, and they walked off towards Victoria Street, where the two street-wise children took the naive-looking David through a hoarding which surrounded an unfinished building. Robert and Sam called this place the Rafts, because of the huge foot-deep pool of rainwater that filled the basement. There were a few children already playing on the building site, but as soon as these 'witnesses' left, several hours later, Robert and Sam made David walk along an iron girder 12 feet above the pool. The boy was too scared to walk across, so Sam and Robert decided to push him off it. He landed with a splash, badly bruised. The sadistic duo then made David get up on to the girder again and once more pushed him off. This time they stripped him of his clothes and boots as he came out of the water. Then they took him even higher up the building, on to a ledge, and pushed him again. This time David Eccles hit the shallow pool and didn't get up, and to make sure he was dead, Sam Crawford knelt on his head as he lay under water. The two children watched the body for two hours, 'to see if it moved' then divided the spoils. They dried the murdered boys wet clothes on a street brazier, then Robert Shearon went home.

On the following day, a group of lads were playing football on a piece of wasteland on Stanley Street, when one of them kicked the ball over the hoarding in Victoria Street. One of them went to get the ball, and found the naked body of David Eccles, lying in a foot of rainwater in the basement pit. Initially, the police thought the unknown boy had drowned whilst bathing, but when Robert's mother read of the tragedy in the newspapers, and learned about the child's clothes being unaccounted for, she realised where her son had obtained his new shirt and boots, and went to the police. The murdered boy's parents later identified the body.

Robert Shearon made a full confession, as did Sam Crawford. In Court, the heads of the children barely reached the level of the dock, and they giggled as they gave their damning testimony, as if they didn't realise the enormity of their crime. The jury returned a verdict of 'wilful murder' against both prisoners, but the boys were acquitted on account of their youth. Their tearful mothers consented to the boys being sent away to a home.

MURDER IN THE FOG

The following murder case, which is still unsolved, is one of the most baffling incidents in criminal history. It contains enough red herrings and twists and turns to tax the mind of Sherlock Holmes himself.

On the day of the murder Liverpool was enveloped in a dense, freezing fog that had lingered over the city for days and seemed to be thickening by the hour. On the Wednesday morning of 20 December 1961, at eight o'clock, 33-year-old Brian Dutton took a cup of tea upstairs to his wife, who was in bed, then left his semi-detached home at 14 Thingwall Lane, Knotty Ash, and embarked on a long and hazardous journey to Widnes, where he worked as a research chemist for ICI.

At home were his 27-year-old wife Maureen Ann Dutton and his two sons, David, aged two, and a 22-day-old baby who had not yet been christened.

Mrs Dutton wanted to take David to see the Christmas crib at Childwall Parish Church, and around 11am, when her mother-in-law called at the house, she asked her if she would babysit while she took her son to the church. Her mother-in-law said she would be able to look after the baby in the afternoon and left the house around midday. However, at 1.30pm Mrs Dutton's mother-in-law phoned from her home at 69 Broadgreen Road to cancel, saying she would not be able to come after all, because of the thick fog.

Around 6.10pm Mr Dutton, having arrived home to find the house in darkness, discovered his wife lying dead on the sitting-room floor. She had been stabbed to death. In a dazed state Mr Dutton called his neighbours in and quickly summoned a doctor.

In the morning room the family's lunch lay half eaten on the table and there was nothing to indicate that a struggle had taken place. Nothing had been stolen and there were no signs of a forced entry. For Mr Dutton, the next traumatic experience, after discovering his wife's body, was finding little David in the living-room. He was upset and appeared to have witnessed the murder, although he and his baby brother had not been harmed.

The police were called and immediately launched an intensive roadcheck of all vehicles in the area, but it yielded nothing.

Chief Superintendent James Morris, head of Liverpool CID, led the investigation into what would subsequently be referred to in the newspapers as the 'Knotty Ash Murder', and Old Swan Police Station became the murder squad headquarters. After examining the murder scene, Morris mustered a hundred detectives with tracker dogs and co-ordinated a search of the Knotty Ash area. The frozen ground in the rear garden of the Duttons' home was raked in the search for the murder weapon, and a squad of Liverpool Corporation workmen probed the drains of Thingwall Lane. In a statement to the press, Chief Superintendent Morris appealed to bus conductors on the nearby Thomas Lane route to contact the police if they had noticed anyone acting in a suspicious manner while boarding a bus between 1.30 and 6.30pm on the day of the murder.

At noon the following day, Mr Herbert Balmer, the deputy chief constable of Liverpool, visited the house with several detectives, a photographer and a fingerprint expert. During their examination of the house, an auxiliary postman called to deliver several Christmas cards. He too was asked if he had noticed anyone suspicious in the area around the time of the killing. He hadn't.

Meanwhile the only witness to the Knotty Ash Murder, little David Dutton – who was now staying with his younger brother at his grandmother's home at Broadgreen Road – was being kept under constant observation by a policewoman. Attempts had been made to question the two-year-old about the events he had witnessed, but the child was largely incoherent. Still, the policewoman listened to his babble for clues.

Chief Superintendent Morris racked his brains in order to fathom possible motives for the fatal stabbing, but could find none. The major questions remained unanswered. Mrs Dutton had been stabbed 14 times in a frenzied attack by someone she had apparently admitted into the house; did this mean the killer was someone known to the murdered woman? Robbery was evidently not the motive, for nothing had been stolen. And why was there no sign of a struggle?

A basic reconstruction of the murder was put together from the forensic examinations. It appeared that Mrs Dutton had forcibly retreated from the front door with a knife pressed against her throat. She had staggered backwards across the hall and into the living-room, where she was killed in front of her son David.

Morris gave a lot of thought to the victim-knew-the-killer theory, and via another press statement urged everyone who had known the murdered woman since her marriage in April 1958 to come forward.

In response to the police appeal to the bus conductors on the Thomas Lane route, a piece of information emerged that seemed to be the breakthrough Morris was hoping for. At 4.30 on the afternoon of the murder, a woman boarded the Number 10d bus en route from Longview to the city centre in East Prescot Road, opposite Eaton Road. She was in an agitated state and out of breath, as if she had been running for quite a distance. In an Irish accent she muttered to herself that she had to get out of Liverpool immediately, and was going to London to catch a plane. She got off the bus at Lime Street and throughout the journey was heard to mumble repeatedly, 'Oh my God! Oh my God!' The woman was described as tall and buxom, and between 25 and 35 years old. She was wearing a pale pink coat, black shoes with stiletto heels and was carrying a white 'envelope' type of bag.

As Morris pondered the report of the Irish woman, the search for the murder weapon – thought to be a narrow-bladed knife – was getting into full swing. An inch-by-inch search of the area around Thingwall Lane produced nothing; the grounds of Thingwall Hall Mental Home were probed with mine detectors until dark; and in the nearby fields detectives working shoulder to shoulder used forks to examine the long grass. But all their efforts proved in vain.

Back at the murder house a detective discovered a light brown leather knife sheath, which Mr Dutton said did not belong to the family. The sheath appeared to be homemade and measured five-and-a-half inches in length and one-and-a-half inches in width.

By this time another piece of information had come to light that offered a plausible motive for the killing of Maureen Dutton. On the day before the murder, a woman, who, like Mrs Dutton, had recently given birth, was at her home in Halewood when a man professing to be a doctor called to examine her. The doctor's appearance and general demeanour gained the young woman's confidence; but when her husband later discovered that there was no doctor in the area with the name given by the man, he quickly informed the police. The bogus doctor was described as dark with a broad nose and cropped curly hair. He wore horn-rimmed spectacles and a dark grey overcoat, and was aged between 27 and 30.

Was he the cowardly fiend who had come out of the fog to call at the home of Maureen Dutton, pretending to be a doctor wanting to examine her? Had Mrs Dutton been murdered by him after she had seen through his perverted disguise? Morris was considering the bogus doctor theory when the line of inquiry shifted once again. Several residents interviewed during the continuing house-to-house enquiries in the area claimed that a suspicious-looking young stranger in a leather jacket had been seen walking along Thingwall Lane towards Thomas Lane at about 1.50pm on the day of the murder.

All Christmas leave for the policemen working on the Dutton case was cancelled. As the door-to-door enquiries continued, detectives heard more and more about the young man in the black leather jacket. Other interviews, however, were being conducted along another line. Morris and Balmer questioned many people who had visited the home of the dead woman over the past few years, and as a result of these interviews, the course of their investigations suddenly took a bizarre twist. Morris and Balmer apparently believed that members of a South Seas cult had been at the Dutton home in recent months and hypothesised that Mrs Dutton could have been the victim of a ritual murder.

Balmer and other detectives read up on the activities of the disciples of the Polynesian god Tiki, and discovered that worshippers made sacrifices to Tiki during the winter solstice – and Mrs Dutton had been murdered during this period. At the beginning of the 1960s the Polynesian cult had a considerable following in Britain and there were many members in Liverpool; so Balmer and several other detectives called at the homes of known members and at the many coffee bars and nightclubs throughout the city which the disciples were known to frequent. Detectives even visited record shops and listened to Polynesian music.

Once again the investigation appeared to have reached a dead end – until 4 January 1962, when a 24-year-old male nurse living in Upper Parliament Street was arrested and charged with the theft of drugs and surgical equipment from three Liverpool hospitals. He was also suspected of having masqueraded as a doctor. The police thought they had collared their man at last, especially since he had a tattoo on his right arm depicting a reversed swastika – the identification mark of a Tiki-worshipper. However, during the trial at Liverpool City Magistrates Court, Rex Makin (for the nurse) poured cold water on the police's hopes. He told the court that the only drugs his client had taken had been sleeping pills, mild sedatives and vitamin K tablets. He also added that the defendant was a man of good character who had never been in trouble before. The nurse had merely had the 'disadvantage of having a tattoo mark on his arm which had led the police to think he might be connected with the murder of Maureen Dutton.'

The male nurse was eliminated from the murder inquiry and the search for the bogus doctor resumed. The police were back at square one.

In the meantime, the search for the elusive murder

weapon in the drains of Knotty Ash and Dovecot resulted in the recovery of about one hundred knives of all types, scissors and even an old bayonet, but the murder weapon was not among them.

By 17 January police had amassed 20,000 statements, and one mysterious figure kept resurfacing among all the data: the young man in the black leather jacket. Despite an intensive appeal in the newspapers, the much-sought youth never came forward to account for his whereabouts on that foggy afternoon. On 18 January the *Liverpool Echo* made a unique contribution to the police investigation by printing a colour identikit picture of the man in the leather jacket on the newspaper's front page. By the following day more than 60 people had come forward to tell the police that they thought they recognised the likeness. Many were mistaken, of course, but some filled in several interesting details about the youth. One woman said she saw a youth in a shiny black jacket on the afternoon of the murder being violently sick at the Methodist Church near the corner of Court Hey Avenue and Greystone. All the time the youth was vomiting, he kept his hands in his pockets for some reason.

Another woman, who lived only a stone's throw from Thingwall Lane, gave a chilling account of how a youth in a leather jacket called at her house on the day of the Dutton murder a short time before 1.50pm. As the woman opened the door, she was confronted by a youth who looked identical to the one in the identikit picture issued by police. He just stood on the doorstep without speaking, with a half-smile on his face, tapping his left hand with his right. Before slamming the door on the stranger, the woman noticed that the youth's hands were well-kept and suntanned, and that he had long slender fingers.

The months rolled by without any more leads; in desperation the police even sought the aid of Interpol. But it was useless. The murderer of Maureen Ann Dutton could not be found. Gradually, the newspaper columns on the case got smaller and smaller and today the case remains a mere puzzler for students of crime.

Perhaps the Knotty Ash Murder resulted from a botched housebreaking attempt. Maybe the youth in the leather jacket was a housebreaker, visiting Knotty Ash under the ideal cover of the fog. The area was then a fairly affluent suburb and Thingwall Lane was a residential street populated by professional and retired people. It is quite plausible that the agitated blonde woman with the Irish accent who boarded the 10d bus that afternoon was the housebreaker's look-out. Perhaps she had panicked at seeing her partner-in-crime emerge from the house spattered in blood. Perhaps the youth knocked on the door of Maureen Dutton's home and expected no answer, and was taken by surprise when someone came to the door.

But there is a problem here. Even if the intruder was confronted by a woman, why should he stab her to death instead of fleeing back into the fog? How could he have been certain that none of Mrs Dutton's family or friends was at the house that afternoon?

Another possibility is that the murderer had no specific motive for killing because he or she was insane. A very short walk away from the scene of the crime there was a home for the mentally ill. Around the time of the murder this institution had only recently been established in a building that had once been the site of St Edward's Orphanage. When the changeover occurred it was a very low-key affair and many of the local residents were not aware that the old orphanage now housed mentally ill patients. A coalman who delivered to St Edward's around the time of the Dutton murder told me that the patients at the home were only restrained from wandering off into Thingwall Lane by a wooden fence a mere three feet high. Is it possible that a patient with a violent streak could have acquired a knife and slipped off the premises to kill at random? I very much doubt this. I believe the answer lies in another direction.

For several years I corresponded with Brian Dutton, the husband of Maureen Dutton – who was actually known to Brian and most who knew her as Ann – her second name. Brian was very helpful and understanding when I asked detailed questions regarding the events of that day and even the layout of his home at the time (Brian even drew a schematic plan of the house for me). Brian also showed me copies of the many letters he had received from couples across the UK who had read of his tragic loss and had offered to adopt his children. I was pleased to hear that David and Andrew, Brian's sons, had done very well for themselves in life.

I feel certain that the killer of Maureen Ann Dutton knew her well, and may have even loved her once, but I feel that his love was unrequited. How did the killer know his victim was alone that day? I believe he knew Mr Dutton was at work because he watched him leave, and the killer would also have known Brian's mother had left the house earlier that day as well. I conducted a lot of research along these lines and discovered that a man had known Maureen from around 1959, when she was starting at Liverpool University, and not long after the Knotty Ash Murder, this man committed suicide. I will present my theory one day when I have undertaken more research, and I must emphasise, it is only a theory.

Around 2002, a man telephoned me at BBC Radio Merseyside (after I had discussed the Knotty Ash Murder on air) to say that his friend had been the elusive youth in the leather jacket and green pullover on Thingwall Lane who had remained beyond the reach of the Liverpool police and even the agents of Interpol. According to the caller, his friend had a valid reason for being in the area of the murder that day. He was delivering bread and his van had broken down because of the cold weather. When this young man later learned that the police were looking for a man who matched his description, he got rid of the jacket and pullover because he knew that Herbert Balmer, the deputy chief constable of Liverpool, had something of an alleged unsavoury reputation for fitting people up when the real culprits to a crime could not be found. That is what I was told, and the caller seemed to be quite old and sounded genuine.

THE CRANBORNE ROAD MURDER

One of the biggest arguments against a death penalty is that innocent people have been hanged in the past. We only have to think of individuals such as Timothy Evans, Derek Bentley and Hussein Mattan, to name but a few who were hanged, but later posthumously pardoned. In the judicial hall of infamy there are numerous examples of gross miscarriages of justice such as the Birmingham Six, the Guildford Four, Sheila Bowler, Stefan Kiszko; the list goes on and on. In Liverpool in the early 1950s, two young men were hanged for a murder in the Wavertree area, and I believe the duo were innocent of the crime. First, here are the facts regarding this controversial murder case.

On the Sunday evening of 19 August 1951, 54-year-old widow, Beatrice Alice Rimmer, left her son's house in Madryn Street, Toxteth. The time was 9.45pm, and Mrs Rimmer walked to the bus stop on High Park Street, accompanied by her son Thomas. In her white net-gloved hands, Mrs Rimmer carried a bunch of flowers, given to her by her son, and an old umbrella which she carried whenever she paid such social visits, more out of habit than necessity, on what had been such a clement sunny day.

The widow soon boarded a Number 27 bus that took her to Lodge Lane, where she stepped down outside the Pavilion Theatre. She then walked down Smithdown Road to her terraced home at Number 7 Cranborne Road, arriving home around 10.10pm. It must have seemed like the end to a rather pleasant day for Mrs Rimmer. She had chatted to her son and played with her lovable little grand-daughter Charmion. All grandmothers love their grandchildren, but Mrs Rimmer absolutely revered Charmion, and, unknown to the child's parents, Beatrice had even made provisions for the toddler in her will. And so, Mrs Rimmer entered her home that Sunday evening after a lovely day, thankfully unaware that she would soon die in a most horrific and brutal way, just seconds after stepping into her hallway.

On the following evening Thomas Rimmer travelled to his mother's house, but before he reached the front door, Mrs Rimmer's neighbour, Jack Grossman, approached him and drew his attention to the milk bottle on the front doorstep and a folded newspaper protruding from the letterbox. The milk bottle had been there since around six in the morning, and this had struck Mr Grossman as very unusual, as Mrs Rimmer was usually an early riser. Thomas Rimmer, being a former policeman (who had resigned from the force a few months before to take up a new occupation, but had now decided to rejoin the Liverpool police), certainly thought the milk bottle and unread newspaper were ominous indications that something was grossly amiss in his mother's home, and he hammered on the door of Number 7 but to no avail. So he removed the newspaper and looked through the letterbox to see what initially looked like a bundle of clothes behind the front door.

Thomas then went to the back of the house and climbed over the wall. The bottom pane of the kitchen window had been broken, yet strangely, Thomas noted that the glass shards were on the floor of the yard, outside the house – as if the window had been broken from inside. The jagged-rimmed hole in the pane was too small for him to climb through, so Thomas carefully used his elbow to enlarge it by knocking in a few shards around the hole. He then climbed in through the widened space into the kitchen.

He walked into the dark hallway, and by the diffused daylight from the curtained window of the front door, Thomas Rimmer saw his mother lying in a large pool of clotted blood She lay just behind the front door, face down, with her head towards him, and stretched out in such a way that her right foot was underneath the old upright hallway chair to the right of the door. The umbrella was still looped around her wrist and the bunch of flowers her son had given her the day before lay wilting beside her.

The widow had died from an extremely violent attack of 20 to 30 blows that had left her with 15 wounds. The police were baffled by the motive behind the crime, because nothing had been stolen from the house, and even the gas and electric meters were untouched. One of the first targets of the housebreakers and burglars in those days was to raid such shilling meters, which provided instant untraceable money. Everything was, to use the phrase of one investigating detective, 'as clean as a new pin' – and that was the way house-proud Mrs Rimmer had always kept her home.

A full-scale police investigation was launched with teams of detectives working round the clock, but Liverpool Police soon reached a dead end – until Chief Superintendent Herbert Balmer suddenly claimed that a man serving time for a burglary at Walton Prison had told him who had committed the Cranborne Road murder: two Mancunians: George Alfred Burns, aged 21, and 22-year-old Edward Devlin.

Chief Superintendent Balmer alleged – rather unrealistically to say the least – that Burns and Devlin had been half-way through a burglary in Manchester (robbing a blinds factory) when they suddenly decided – for some unfathomable motive which was never explained by Balmer – to travel 36 miles to Liverpool to carry out a burglary at Mrs Rimmer's home.

Group B bloodstains found on the clothing belonging to one of the men was cited as evidence – even though it was not of the same blood-group as Mrs Rimmer, who was Group A. The blood cited as evidence of involvement in the Rimmer murder was in fact blood acquired from a pub brawl, in which Burns and Devlin had been involved. When the murder trial opened at St George's Hall, Rose Heilbron Q.C. defended Devlin, and Sir Noel Goldie Q.C. defended Burns. Lord Justice Finnemore heard the case, and it soon became apparent that the evidence against Burns and Devlin was purely circumstantial – no one had seen them enter or leave the house on Cranborne Road, and no fingerprints had been found at the scene of the crime. All the same, the two men were subsequently found guilty of Mrs Rimmer's murder.

When the verdict was announced, a wave of sighs and startled gasps filled the court, with one woman in the public gallery even screaming out 'Oh, no … no! Never!'

The entire case and the charges had seemed so phoney and flimsy, that everyone, even Burns and Devlin, had expected a Not Guilty verdict, and so they treated the whole affair as if it were a joke. They smiled and giggled and never expected in a million years to be hanged on such contradictory and shaky testimony from so-called witnesses – when even the forensic evidence proved that they were not involved. And yet, they were found guilty, and sentenced to hang side by side at Walton Goal.

When the verdict of guilty was announced by the foreman of the jury, Devlin told the judge in a broken voice, 'My Lord, I would like to stress that it means the police are not infallible to tell lies.' And Burns also had something to say. He looked up at the public gallery and said the judge had given a prejudiced view of the case. Burns then turned to face the 12 people of the jury who had sentenced himself and his friend to death by hanging, and told them: 'I cannot understand how you brought a verdict of a guilty. It is a most unfair verdict.'

Judge Finnemore then put on the black cap and in a monotone voice, he pronounced the sentence of death as women cried openly in the gallery.

Only now did this matter appear serious to Burns and Devlin. Only now had the penny dropped. Upon seeing the donning of the black cap they must have realised that they were the victims of a conspiracy. They were being framed, fitted up, for a murder that had taken place 36 miles from their home city – all without a shred of evidence being produced to justify the ultimate punishment.

The two men weren't laughing now as they learned that they would be hanged side by side on Tuesday, 18 March 1952 at Walton Prison.

The doomed Mancunians had one last chance. Rose Heilbron Q.C. went to the Court of Criminal Appeal, appealing against the convictions on the grounds that Justice Finnemore had misdirected the jury. She told the appeal court about the judge's ridiculous assertion about Burns and Devlin murdering Mrs Rimmer and afterwards returning to Manchester to complete the burglary job they had abandoned, and she told the court how it was unlikely for two thieves to break into Mrs Rimmer's home and not disturb or take anything.

Forensic evidence had even shown how none of the drawers or cupboards had been opened in Mrs Rimmer's home on the night of the murder. Despite Miss Heilbron's noble attempt to save the lives of two innocent men, the appeal was dismissed, and a new execution date would now have to be set. The Home Secretary of the day, David Maxwell Fyfe, ordered an inquiry into the murder case, in an effort to unearth new evidence to prove the innocence of the condemned men. Such an inquiry at the eleventh hour was a very bold step to take after the dismissal of Heilbron's appeal. The inquiry came to nothing, and the mothers of Burns and Devlin visited their sons in Walton Gaol. The mothers even sent a telegram to the Queen, begging her to intervene, but no help came.

Just after 9am on the Friday morning of 25 April 1952, Alfie Burns and Teddy Devlin stood side by side on the trapdoor of the gallows in Walton Gaol, each with a white linen bag over his head. The arms of the young men were strapped to their sides, and their legs were also bound together by the ankles. The executioner, Albert Pierrepoint, the most prolific and experienced hangman of the twentieth century, who would go on to hang at least 433 men and 17 women, slipped heavy nooses over their hooded heads and expertly adjusted the large knots into specific submental positions on the necks of the men – under their chins, to ensure a maximum fracture of the upper cervical spine – before stepping back to throw the lever. The trapdoor fell away, and Burns and Devlin fell. They both died within a minute.

I have always believed that the real killer of Mrs Rimmer lived locally and knew the murder victim *intimately*. Whoever killed the widow evidently couldn't wait for Mrs Rimmer to come further into the house, for she was attacked *as soon as she set foot inside her home*. It's as if the killer was so enraged by her, or something she had done, he had acted in an emotional frenzied state. If the murderer had wanted to know where the woman kept her savings (and Mrs Rimmer kept no savings or valuables at her home incidentally), he only had to lie in wait in the front parlour or the kitchen before pouncing on her with a knife, but instead he attacks Mrs Rimmer inches from her front door, thus running many risks of immediate detection. A passer-by or a neighbour could have heard the widow cry out or scream on such a typically quiet suburban Sunday evening.

The police found three sweet wrappers in Mrs Rimmer's kitchen near the broken window. On one of these wrappers the brand name read: 'Santus Super Sweets', and on another wrapper the words 'Taverner and Routledge' – a local sweet firm. The third sweet wrapper was blank. Mrs Rimmer was a scrupulously clean woman, and wouldn't have left those sweet wrappers lying about, so we must assume that the killer, or killers, ate sweets in that kitchen before the murder was committed. No one in their right mind would commit a brutal murder, then wait around eating sweets. When detectives calculated how small the hole in the kitchen window had been before Thomas Rimmer enlarged it, they decided that the murderer had either been exceptionally slim, or had in fact entered the house through the front door and created the hole in the window for some reason, possibly to mislead the police. The brick which was probably used to smash the window pane was found in the backyard, and had no fingerprints on it. Detectives also noticed that there were no traces of Mrs Rimmer's Group A blood in the kitchen, as if the killer had escaped via the front door. Most of the glass from the broken kitchen window was, as I have described, found in the yard, which leads me to believe that the murderer broke the window from the inside to make it look as if the killer had gained access to the house via the kitchen window. This would mean that the person had, in reality, entered the house with a key. So what person would have such a key? Was Mrs Rimmer seeing a man who had perhaps obtained a key from her?

Neighbours of the dead woman described her as a shy and retiring person who never discussed her business with anyone, so it's difficult to discover if she was seeing anyone in a romantic capacity. Mrs Rimmer was a well-known and well-liked member of the Dovedale Ladies' Bowling Club, which was based in Wavertree Playground, although she rarely went on outings with this club. A Mrs Liggett, the secretary of the bowling club said that in the two years before Mrs Rimmer's shocking death, the widow had not turned up as frequently as she used to at the club, and had claimed to have been ill, and yet the murder victim's son, Thomas, said his mother had been in fine health during that time.

Mrs Rimmer was also fond of whist, and often went on outings with the Sefton Park Conservative Club to various pleasant venues to indulge in her card games with both men and women. In an article in the *Liverpool Echo* printed just after the murder, a woman described as a friend, says of Mrs Rimmer: 'It has been said that Mrs Rimmer was a recluse and never went out at night, but this is far from being the truth. She went out on a whist drive on most nights. She seemed very happy and jolly when I last saw her.'

I had relatives living in the vicinity of the murdered woman's home at the time of the baffling killing, and they heard the intriguing rumour that Alice Rimmer was seeing someone connected with the local Conservative Club, and that she had become attached to this man after being celibate for a short while after the death of her husband, Thomas Woosey Rimmer, who passed away (from a cerebral haemhorrage) in July 1950 – just 13 months before his wife's murder. The mysterious man who is thought to have been seeing Mrs Rimmer is said to have lived less than two hundred yards away from Cranborne Road in a neighbouring street off Lawrence Road. Could this man have committed a crime of passion for reasons that are still unknown to us? If this was the case, it would certainly make sense of the following obscure fact, recorded by the renowned police forensic expert Dr J B Firth.

At the Rimmer murder trial, Firth told how he had found some locks of hair that had been cut from Alice Rimmer's head after the murder, and he was at a loss to explain why. The prosecution were trying to maintain that Burns and Devlin had simply attacked Mrs Rimmer because she had entered her home as they had just come into the house through the kitchen window, and yet the police had spoken of three sweet wrappers being found in the kitchen which did not belong to the woman, and these wrappers did not have fingerprints upon them to connect them to the accused men or to Mrs Rimmer. A very questionable witness, produced by Herbert Balmer, claimed to have seen Devlin with a bloodstained handkerchief wrapped around his hand, which had been injured when he supposedly broke the kitchen window. And yet, there were no finger prints found anywhere in the house to connect Burns or Devlin with the crime, and if the two young men had worn gloves, how would they have cut their hands on the kitchen window? And why on earth would they cut a lock of hair from Mrs Rimmer's head after the murder, before climbing back through a hole in a kitchen window that was so small that Mrs Rimmer's son had to enlarge it? How on earth would two Manchester men know that Mrs Rimmer was out that Sunday night, and how could they be entirely sure she wouldn't return home with someone? This hints at inside knowledge, but the police never took up this line of inquiry, and instead, two innocent young men were hanged for somebody else's crime.

In 2003, I gave a talk on Jack the Ripper to over 3,000 people at St George's Hall, and after the talk, I was visited by several people, many of them with stories about supernatural experiences they'd had. One man, who looked to be about 75 to perhaps 80 years of age, approached me, and offered me a silver locket containing an oval black and white portrait of a beautiful young lady. Facing this oval photograph, in the lid of the locket, there was a coiled lock of dark hair. The old man asked me: 'Can you get anything from that?'

He believed I was psychic, and I told him that I wasn't; I merely collected supernatural stories from the public. The old man then said he had been in love with the woman depicted in the locket in her later years, and that she had had an affair behind her husband's back, but 13 months after her husband died, the woman had been murdered. The old man seemed to have tears in his eyes as he related this information to me. A group of people impatiently stepped forward, wanting me to sign a bundle of my *Haunted Liverpool* books, and I think the old man said goodbye and left. I lost sight of him soon afterwards in the crowds of St George's Hall, and I did not for one moment think that he was talking about the victim of the Cranborne Road Murder until many years later when I decided to research the case. I came upon an early photograph of Mrs Rimmer when she was barely out of her teens, and realised it was the same photograph of the woman in that locket I had been shown by the old man in 2003. That locket he had handed me had contained a lock of hair; the killer of Mrs Rimmer had taken clippings of her hair as she lay in her hallway that fateful Sunday night.

All I recall is that the old man was as tall as me – about six feet two – and had grayish blue eyes. He did not speak in a local accent, but in a rather refined manner. He was bald, with patches of white hair on each side of his head, and dressed immaculately in a dark blue suit. I also seem to recollect that he carried a walking cane. Perhaps he was merely a relative or former friend of Mrs Rimmer, or perhaps he was the man who took her life. He may still be alive.

MURDER ON THE HIGH SEAS

It was in the month of April, 1857, when a gentle but slow-witted seaman named Andrew Rose joined the crew of the barque *Martha and Jane*, which was anchored off Barbados. It didn't take Captain Henry Rogers long to discover that the new member of his crew was easy prey, and he and his fawning cronies, William Miles (first mate) and Charles Seymour (second mate), soon had it in for Rose.

Seymour gave Rose a simple task to perform on the ship, but wasn't satisfied with the way the new recruit set about his job, so he punched and kicked him until he was black and blue. After that savage and gratuitous beating, several members of the crew took pity on Rose and urged him to run away; Rose took their advice. But shortly afterwards was recaptured by the police and taken back to the *Martha and Jane*, where he was put in irons.

Now Captain Rogers had a genuine excuse to unleash his brutal nature; and shortly after the barque set sail for the port of Liverpool, Rose was mercilessly thrashed by him and the first and second mates. They kicked him and whipped him with a length of rope until they were exhausted, leaving the poor lad's body a swollen blood-soaked mess.

And the cruelty didn't stop there. Days later, the shackled Rose started singing a hymn when Captain Rogers appeared on deck. The captain instructed the first mate to fetch him a large iron bolt, which he then rammed into Rose's mouth. Miles and Seymour made sure the bolt, which was threatening to choke Rose, was kept securely in place by tying a strong length of yarn around Rose's head. Well pleased with their sport, the sadistic captain and his henchmen forced Rose to endure this ordeal for an hour-and-a-half before removing the bolt.

Another of the captain's perverted little pleasures was to set his dog on to Rose with the command 'Bite that man!' And the dog would charge at the unfortunate mariner and literally tear off chunks of his flesh. Many of the bite wounds sustained by Rose later became infected and ran with pus. But Rose's state of health didn't prevent the captain from sending him naked up the mast to furl the sail, with the first mate following behind with a whip. More sickeningly still, the captain would often make Rose eat his own excrement.

When the ship was a week out from Liverpool, Captain Rogers was standing on deck, surveying the pathetic sore-covered body of Andrew Rose when, with an expression of contempt on his weather-beaten face, he suddenly said: 'Rose, I wish you would either drown or hang yourself.' Rose had endured enough, and did not care any more; he wanted to be rid of his terrible suffering, and so replied: 'I wish you would do it for me.'

Rogers reacted venomously to the mildly audacious act of insubordination; he and the two mates grabbed Rose by the arms and dragged him to the mainmast. A rope was produced and a noose was made. They put the noose over Rose's head and hanged him from the mainmast for two minutes. At the end of this time, Rose's eyes were bulging, and his protruding tongue was starting to turn black. The captain gave the order to release him, and Rose fell to the deck with a thump and lay there, inert and barely alive.

'If I'd kept him there just half a minute longer, he'd have been a goner!' Captain Rogers declared to his crew without a trace of compassion.

The terrifying ordeal proved too much for Rose, and shortly afterwards, on 5 June, after struggling up on to the deck in a semi-conscious state, he cried out one last time, then died. The crew found the sight and stench of Rose's ulcerated and maggot-infested body unbearable and so Captain Rogers ordered it to be thrown into the sea.

Four days later the *Martha and Jane* arrived at Liverpool, and several members of the crew immediately reported Captain Rogers and his mates to the authorities. Rogers and his two partners in crime were taken into custody, and at St George's Hall on 19 August 1857 they were tried for the murder of Andrew Rose. The jury found them guilty, and when word of the verdict reached the huge mob assembled outside the building, Lime Street echoed to the sound of jubilant cheering. Captain Henry Rogers, William Miles and Charles Edward Seymour were all sentenced to death, but the two mates were later reprieved.

The hitherto callous and brutal personality of Captain Rogers apparently underwent a dramatic change while he awaited execution in his cell at Kirkdale Gaol. He turned to God and prayed almost constantly through his final lonely days and nights.

On 12 September, at noon, the captain who had taken sadistic delight in torturing a simple-minded man and robbing him of his life, sampled some of the fear that Andrew Rose had felt under his wicked hand when he was taken to the scaffold in full view of a 30,000-strong crowd of laughing and jeering spectators. Until the white cap was pulled over his face by the hangman, Rogers stood on the gallows erected near the top of the prison wall and stared out at the sea's horizon, beyond the crowd below, beyond Liverpool Bay. The eternal sea was the last thing the captain saw. The sea that had been his life – and Andrew Rose's watery grave.

After the hanging a subscription was opened for the widow and five children of Captain Rogers, and £670 was collected – a substantial sum in those days.

SOME BAFFLING BOOTLE MYSTERIES

There are a great many criminological mysteries concerning Bootle that seem determined to remain unsolved. Take for example, the mysterious death of 18-year-old Bootle shop assistant Laura Millicent Benson, on 26 July 1929, at Stanley Hospital, whilst being treated for a goitre (a slight swelling in her neck). Coroner G C Mort discovered that Miss Benson's death had been due to poisoning by arsenic, but just how this arsenic was administered to the girl was never discovered. Since Christmas 1928, Miss Benson had complained of a large swelling on her neck, along with feelings of nausea, and a doctor had diagnosed the lump as a goitre, but thought it would perhaps disappear in time.

The girl went to the local park one day with her father (a retired policeman) because it was thought that the fresh air would do her 'the world of good'. Fresh air was recommended for every ailment in those days, but whilst in the park, the girl's condition worsened. She told her father she felt as if she was on fire, and tore off her coat and shirt because of an agonising burning sensation in her chest. In February Miss Benson weighed ten stone and 16 pounds, but by early April her weight had plummeted to just eight stone. Around this time, Laura was seen to be taking a dark medicine from two brown bottles, which the coroner produced at the inquest. This mysterious medicine contained a tiny amount of arsenic. Just who gave Miss Benson the two bottles was never discovered. Laura's mother said her daughter had eaten the same food as the rest of the family, and no one else had suffered any ill effects.

Detective-inspector Carter of the Bootle Borough Police took the two medicine bottles found in possession of Laura Benson before she was admitted to hospital, and had them analysed, together with a box containing tablets prescribed by a doctor. City Analyst, Professor W H Roberts, had the bottles of medicine analysed, and discovered that if the girl had drunk a whole bottle of the medicine, she would still have only ingested the equivalent of a quarter of a grain of arsenic, and Laura had not even drunk half of a bottle – so what was the source of the arsenic poisoning?

The coroner obtained samples of wallpaper from the girl's room, as such paper contained tiny amounts of the poison back in that era, but he discovered that Laura could not have been poisoned in any way from the wallpaper. Summing up, the coroner told the court that the girl had died from arsenic poison; that the arsenic had been taken by her through the mouth, but in several doses. The jury agreed with the coroner, and returned a verdict that Laura Millicent Benson had died from a poisonous dose of arsenic taken ten to fourteen days before her death, but that the evidence as to how she came to be suffering from arsenical poisoning was not clear, and today, the girl's death remains a mystery.

I believe the girl was deliberately poisoned by someone; perhaps a doctor who hid a psychopathic streak behind an otherwise respectable persona, or perhaps even a pharmacist. We'll probably never know the truth now.

Another unsolved Bootle murder concerns the fate of the founder of the Bibby shipping line, John Bibby of Linacre, after whom Bibby's Lane was named. Mr Bibby, the son of an Eccleston farmer, began as a humble businessman who sold iron in Liverpool, and when he married the heiress Mary Mellard, his newfound wealth enabled him to embark on more ambitious ventures, the first of which was merely a share in a sailing ship called *Dove*. Bibby slowly acquired more shares, and then acquired ships of his own and gradually he came to own his own postal ships, carrying mail and parcels between Parkgate and Dublin, but it wasn't long before Bibby's ambitions pushed his ventures further afield – to ports in Bombay, the Baltic, South America and even China. Bibby shipped textiles and manufactured goods to the world, and the returning ships came home with their cargo holds crammed with tea, silk, sugar, spices, coffee, molasses, wood, cotton and rum.

Bibby's wealth mushroomed by the month, and one 300-ton ship that returned to Liverpool was so packed with exotic goods, it took stevedores three months to unload her. Bibby became the most famous merchant in the town, and a major shareholder in the Royal Bank of Liverpool. Then, one evening in summer of 1840, it all came to an abrupt end.

Bibby, who was now 56, went to a bank shareholders' meeting in Liverpool on 17 July 1840 and after discussing business, he dined with his friends and other merchants. Around 11.15 that July night, a coachman named Henry Simpson was waiting at his stand on Castle Street in the centre of Liverpool, when he saw two businessmen come out of the Royal Bank of Liverpool on Dale Street. The duo was John Bibby and his friend Mr Taylor. The two men got into Simpson's coach, and Mr Bibby told the driver to take his friend to the top of Everton Hill, but Mr Taylor told the driver Simpson to stop upon reaching the bottom of the hill, and he walked the rest of the way home. Bibby told the driver to then take him to the gate of the Primrose Hotel in Bootle, which Simpson did, and when he reached this destination, the coachman got down from his vehicle and asked Bibby: 'Which is your house sir?'

Mr Bibby said, 'I know where I am now; set me down; I shall do very well.'

After paying the coachman seven shillings, Bibby walked steadily down a narrow secluded lane, and although he had been drinking a bit too much (as Simpson had ascertained from the way the merchant had swayed when first getting into the coach) he walked in a straight line into the darkness. Henry Simpson then drove home to Batt Street, Everton, arriving there around 1am. His wife and six children were sound asleep, and he stabled his horses. He found the supper his wife had left out for him by the fire, ate it, had a drink, then retired.

On the following morning at 2pm, Henry Ambrose, a farmer residing in Stand Park in the parish of Sefton, near to Aintree Racecourse, was working in his fields, when he noticed the head and shoulders of a man protruding from a flooded pit in an adjoining field. The body was more than 300 yards from any side of the pit. Farmer Ambrose obtained assistance from several men and ventured into the watery pit to get a closer look at the corpse. The hat on the dead man's head had been pushed down hard almost covering his nose. Ambrose and his friends dragged the well dressed corpse out of the pit with a pitchfork, then searched its pockets in an effort to find some article to identify the body, and in doing so they found a bunch of keys, a shilling, a small memorandum book, and a knife.

Papers in the memorandum book contained the name John Bibby, and so the farmer and his friends sent for

Joseph Webster, the constable of Litherland. The constable saw that there was a dent in the left side of Mr Bibby's hat, as if he had been struck there by someone. It was also established that Bibby's hunting watch, which had his initials engraved on its back, was missing from the body.

The post mortem examination on Bibby was carried out by Mr T Wainwright, who stated that he had found marks of violence upon the body in the form of bruises on the left arm, back of the wrist and one on each knee. The mouth and the eyes of the corpse were closed when the body was found with a placid facial expression. Wainwright deduced that Mr Bibby was alive when he fell, or was pushed, into the water, and had died instantly, probably from drowning. Some believed the so-called marks of violence had been caused by the over-eager attempts by Farmer Ambrose and his friends as they dragged the body out of the pit with the pitch-fork, but the coroner said the marks could not have been made after death, when blood is not flowing. Instead, the coroner opined that the marks had been made by the fingers of people who had attacked John Bibby.

The murderer or murderers of Mr Bibby were never brought to justice, but perhaps, somewhere out there, someone will have the murdered merchant's hunting watch, with the long-dead victim's full initials – J J B – upon it. The Bibby family did offer the substantial reward of £500 for the detection or apprehension of those responsible for the murder, and even a Royal Pardon for the culprits was negotiated, but no one was ever charged with the crime. Bibby's four sons inherited their father's highly successful shipping business, and the Bibby name lived on for centuries.

And now, here is another Bootle murder that is still resisting all attempts to be solved.

Every Friday was Bootle day for Harry Baker – the day the jovial 61-year-old Jewish credit draper did a round of calls on housewife customers in the town. However, Friday, 6 June 1958 was a Bootle day with a tragic difference for gentle mild-mannered Harry – a 'perky little sparrow' is how one man described him; the 'club man' who never pushed his customers hard if they could not pay.

Mr Baker, whose home was at Southport, had made about 50 calls on customers in the Bootle area during that morning. He had 63 other calls to make in Bootle and the adjoining north Liverpool district that day. Then he vanished, apparently into thin air. He was last seen alive talking to a thin-faced man at about 1.45pm, at the Number 23 bus stop in Strand Road, Bootle, from where he may have boarded a bus into Liverpool for a swift lunch at a city cafe. There were unconfirmed reports that the club man had been seen walking along rather morosely with his head bowed near the Pier Head, but these uncorroborated accounts were to throw no light on the mystery that was to soon unfold.

Seventeen days after he vanished – on 23 June 1958 – Harry Baker's body was found, amid pink and purple rhododendrons, wrapped in two sacks on a plantation off the main A50 trunk road at High Leigh, near Knutsford, Cheshire. He had been beaten and strangled.

Today, the murder is still unsolved. Where did Harry die and who killed him? What was the motive? Was this murder really committed for the £25 (which the club man was carrying), two watches and a fountain pen, missing from Baker's possession when his body was found? How many people were implicated in the killing?

One of the biggest manhunts Merseyside has ever known was mounted by the police, and at the height of the investigation, 20,000 people were interviewed, 9,000 statements were taken and replies obtained to 10,000 questionnaires. Unfortunately, positive placing of Baker's movements while he was alive came to a dead stop at that Number 23 bus stop.

One theory that was propounded by detectives on the case was that the killer – or killers – had fled abroad, and this led to police checks overseas as the inquiry proceeded. Information still trickled in about the crime from time to time in the years following Baker's murder, but no significant headway was ever made, despite the £500 reward for any information leading to an arrest which was offered by members of the Jewish community in Southport.

Eight years after the murder in 1966, Detective Chief Inspector Bill Cotter, head of the Bootle CID, ruefully remarked to the *Liverpool Echo*: 'The Baker death is still very much in the minds of police officers. The file will, of course, remain open until the killer or killers of this man come to book, even if it takes another eight years.'

Decades on, it looks as if the murderer or murderers of the quiet inoffensive club man loved by all on his rounds will never be brought to justice.

THE HIGH RIP GANG

The Peanut Gang, the Fiveways Gang, the Swallows Gang – Liverpool has had its fair share of criminal gangs over the years, but none of them compare with the High Rip Gang, whose infamy was once known throughout the land.

In 1874, 26-year-old doctor Robert Morgan made an August Bank Holiday trip to New Ferry with his wife and brother. Upon passing a public house in Tithebarn Street, a swaggering young ruffian named McCrave approached him and asked for 'ale money'. McCrave was a notorious member of the much-feared High Rip Gang, a large mob of violent criminals that held North Liverpool in a grip of terror.

Doctor Morgan made the mistake of suggesting that 17-year-old McCrave should work and not beg. McCrave's associates, two thickset teenagers, also aged 17, named Campbell and Mullen, closed in on the physician. They knocked him down with simultaneous punches, then kicked him along the street for 40 feet. His screams for mercy went unheeded, and not a single member of the public came to his aid.

Mrs Morgan almost fainted at the sight of the vicious attack on her husband, and her brother-in-law was equally helpless as other members of the High Rip turned up. By the time the police arrived upon the scene, Doctor Morgan was dying from internal bleeding. It was too late to save him.

In a state of shock, Morgan's brother finally snapped and he suicidally chased after McCrave. The violent ruffian was captured in the brave pursuit when a policeman also gave chase. Although McCrave remained tight-lipped about the identity of his accomplices, it was only a matter of days before Mullen and Campbell were collared and brought into custody. Mullen had been discovered trying to board a ship at the docks.

The brutal death of the respectable Dr Morgan at the hands of the High Rip Gang was reported across the land, and served to darken Liverpool's reputation as a rough city even further. Even hardened criminals in Liverpool lived in fear of the High Rip.

In 1879, tough docker Georgie Yates, of Anfield, once related to a reporter how he had lost an eye and suffered a broken jaw at the hands of two women members of the infamous gang. Both women were barefooted and barely out of their teens, yet they fought like prize fighters when they set upon Yates as they were on a robbing spree from a waterfront warehouse.

Poverty was the mother of crime in the days of the High Rip, and it's plain to see that desperate people in those days often resorted to very desperate measures to survive.

McCrave, Campbell and Mullen were sentenced to death. Their families sent a petition to the Home Secretary, begging him to let the boys off with a flogging, but it was rejected. At the eleventh hour, only one gang member was saved. Campbell was reprieved and given a life sentence because of good behaviour and a rather sudden new-found devotion to the Bible!

The crime had horrified the British public, and justice had to be seen to be done, otherwise there would have been a riot in Liverpool. Most people were enraged at Campbell's reprieve, and there were many petitions for him to be flogged to death. However, the hanging of ringleader McCrave and his right-hand man Mullen on 3 January 1875, served as a warning to the remaining members of the High Rip Gang.

The High Rip later disbanded, and several less ferocious gangs falsely claimed to be splinters of the most evil mob to ever walk Liverpool's mean streets.

In the 1880s, there was a resurgence of several other gangs, and a last-ditch attempt by several members of the criminal underworld in north Liverpool to resurrect the High Rip.

Fortunately a hardliner judge, Mr Justice Day arrived at Liverpool Assizes in 1886 and began to deal severe sentences to the latest members of the reincarnated High Rip Gang, who were holding the north of the city in a grip of fear. Justice Day sentenced six members of the High Rip to be hanged and had other violent criminals flogged unmercifully with the cat-o'-nine-tails.

The darkest hour is before the dawn and before the High Rip Gang was finally smashed, the remaining members put up a vicious fight to regain their territories on Scotland Road.

One windy night in 1889, PC Corrigan staggered into the police bridewell at Cheapside, minus his helmet, jacket and front teeth. He had clotted blood under a broken nose and was out of breath.

The other policemen listened in dread as they sat him down. Between sips of naval rum, Corrigan told them that the High Rip Gang was on the move again and was now taking control of the goods yards and warehouses of the Lancashire and Yorkshire Railway station.

A wool warehouse had also been ransacked and PC James had been thrown into the Leeds-Liverpool canal by a tough, barefooted female member of the gang. Luckily he'd been able to swim to safety. A warehouseman had been coshed and left in a pool of blood and there was a rumour that the gang had their sights on a tobacco warehouse near Great Howard Street.

The police sergeant at the bridewell mustered the men and told them to 'get up there and at them', but the policemen were understandably not too keen. With a police mutiny on the cards, the sergeant rapped the counter with his baton and reminded the men it was their duty to protect the public. At this point, a huge raw newcomer of a policeman, known as Pins, announced: 'I'll bring them in, if none of the others will venture!'

The sergeant shook the oversized hand of the constable, then watched him leave the bridewell alone.

Upon seeing this solitary giant of a policeman strolling up Scotland Road, the ringleader and deputy of the High Rip moved in with their coshes and, as the first one attempted to take a swipe at Pins, the brave policeman threw a punch that dazed the criminal. The Samson in blue then turned him upside down and bashed his head on the cobbles, knocking him clean out. The blow from the other gang member missed his target and hit his unconscious colleague's shin. Pins seized him by the throat and up-ended him in the same way he'd inverted the other blackguard. The High Ripper screamed for mercy, remembering the fate of his upturned partner-in-crime, but Pins laughed and dipped him twice, banging his skull on the cobblestones.

Into the darkness, the High Rippers retreated, confused without their brazen leader. Pins turned and, carrying the unconscious ruffians over each shoulder, whistled merrily and delivered the criminals to the astonished sergeant at Cheapside.

On the following night, Pins up-ended another High Ripper and, in the presence of five other policemen, swung the gangster in an arc, knocking over three other rogues like ninepins.

At the ensuing trial, Pins told Justice Day he could collar six ruffians in a day's work, saying: 'You see, me Lord, I sometimes *pins* them against a wall and slaps them like this or I turn them upside down and tap them on the ground and they come along nice and quiet.'

PC Pins became a folklore character overnight and was the final nail in the coffin of the High Rip Gang.

THE STRANGE FATE OF BLUE LIZZIE

Liverpool is a city of countless ghosts, and many of these earthbound spirits have unfinished business, which ties them to this world of the living. Considering the number of murders in this city, and the sudden severance of life which those crimes often entail, perhaps we should not be too surprised at some of the more gruesome apparitions to be found in haunted Liverpool. The following is just one case in point.

Days before the Christmas of 1965, 37-year-old Jack Terry and his 28-year-old girlfriend Elsie Jones left the Knightsbridge Restaurant in Liverpool's Covent Garden, and stepped into the wintry night air. There was a visitation of pale sleet upon the poorly lit lane, and Jack curled his arm around the smartly-dressed Elsie as they headed towards Water Street. Suddenly, a bluish radiance was visible to the couple, as if a neon sign had been switched on in one of the many dark niches of the lane.

A glowing blue figure of a naked woman stepped out into the path of Jack and Elsie, and at that precise moment a high-pitched bell was struck by someone. Elsie stopped in her tracks and clutched Jack's leather jacket. Jack also halted, more stunned than scared at the sight of the glowing nude with flowing long grey hair and eerie-looking eyes. What was obviously some ghost let out a terrible shriek that the couple would remember for the rest of their lives. The radiant woman ran straight at the couple, and as Elsie yelped and tried to bury her face in Jack's chest, her boyfriend bravely shielded her from the evil-looking spectre.

The face of the phosphorescent ghost twisted into a

horrifying expression of pure hate, and lunged at Jack with her hands held out like claws. He screwed up his eyes, hoping it was all some bad dream, but cried out as ice-cold nails ripped down his face. When he opened his eyes, the terrifying apparition had vanished.

Elsie was hysterical, and as the couple hurried past Oriel Chambers and on to well-lit Water Street, Elsie noticed the long red scratch marks, that started on Jack's forehead and continued below on to his cheeks, right down to his chin. Jack felt the scratches – they stung. He and Elsie rode a taxi to his home in Sunbury Road, Anfield, where Jack's mum treated the scratches. She didn't say anything, but assumed Elsie had inflicted them. Jack told his mum about the ghost but she wouldn't believe him and there was a massive row which ended with Jack staying at Elsie's home in Mildmay Road, Norris Green.

On Christmas Day 1965, at around 5am, a policeman was walking past the Pig and Whistle on Covent Garden when he saw a vagrant lying on his back in the icy road. Above the tramp there was a faint smudge of light, but as the police constable looked on, he saw that the light was in fact a naked woman, unaccountably lit up, and she was leaning over the tramp. 'What's going on there?' shouted the policeman, more out of fear than professional curiosity, and the woman vanished. The tramp told how the ghastly ghost of a woman of about 50 had attacked him and knocked him to the ground. The constable told the vagrant to be on his way.

These attacks continued almost every year, always around Christmas time, and I researched the hauntings, only to make a chilling discovery. On Christmas Day, 1919, 54-year-old prostitute Elizabeth McDermott was strangled, stripped naked, and then somehow drained of every drop of blood on Liverpool's Covent Garden, just around the corner from the Town Hall. At first, suspicion rested on a seaman named John Brien, who happened to be in the wrong place at the wrong time as he sought a woman of the night near Lime Street, but he was soon eliminated from the inquiry.

The killer of Lizzie McDermott, described by one detective as an evil genius, was never caught, and for many years, Lizzie McDermott's ghostly naked form, blue because it was devoid of blood, and with red eyes from blood vessels that had burst with strangulation, was seen prowling the area where she had met a brutal but sinister death.

A Shooting at the Station

Unsolved crimes always fascinate the public. When the professionals can find no solution to account for some lethal deed, the armchair detectives step in and take great delight in propounding their own theories. The following incident, which occurred in 1929, is still unsolved, although many detectives, including the amateur variety, have attempted to piece together the events which led to the tragic shooting of two men in a Cheshire police station.

In April 1929, the Reverend Frank Hayward left his church near Oldham in order to visit his parents in Runcorn. His fiancée, Miss Margaret Mackintosh, the daughter of the Vicar of Oldham, accompanied him on the trip. Frank's 56-year-old father, Charles Hayward, a superintendent in the Cheshire Constabulary, was very proud of his only son and had sacrificed a great deal so that Frank could take holy orders. Frank was the apple of his father's eye, and the superintendent often said that life would be unbearable without a son to take an interest in.

On this particular visit 31-year-old Frank told his devoted father that he planned to marry soon and had ambitions to build a new church in the not-too-distant future. Mr Hayward listened keenly to his son's aspirations, full of admiration.

On this fateful weekend, around eleven, Superintendent Hayward was visiting Runcorn Police Station and he went down into a basement store-room accompanied by the acting sergeant on duty. The store-room contained a number of high-powered rifles, ten revolvers and 397 rounds of ammunition. This hardware had been surrendered to officers over the years, but the firearms were not used by the police. Thinking that some of the hardware in the store-room might interest his son, the superintendent decided to arrange for him to visit the station. At noon he and Frank went down into the store-room. Meanwhile, his fiancée Miss Mackintosh was packing her case in the superintendent's home, which adjoined the station. About ten minutes later, acting Sergeant Bell, who was busy working in the station office, was startled by a loud bang. Shortly afterwards Bell heard the superintendent's voice shouting for him, and he raced down the stairs to the store-room, where he met his superior officer.

'Bell,' said Superintendent Hayward, 'something terrible has happened. My son picked up the revolver. He did not know there was anything in it, and it went off before I knew what had happened.'

Sergeant Bell ran back upstairs to phone for medical help, and on his way he heard another gunshot. Rushing back to the store-room he found the superintendent lying dead with a bullet wound in his head, just above his right ear. The doctor arrived minutes later to find the reverend, who had a gaping bullet hole three inches above his right eye, at the point of death.

People who knew the father and son were convinced that the shooting was not the result of a murder and suicide by the father, nor suicide of the son, followed by the father. In fact Inspector Postons, one of the last people to see Frank Hayward before his death, said the young man had cheerfully told him about his forthcoming marriage and his plans to set up a new parish.

At the inquest into the double tragedy the coroner asked Inspector Postons if anything had been troubling Superintendent Hayward prior to the shooting.

'No, sir. He was of a very cheerful disposition and he was devoted to his son,' replied the inspector.

However, some baffling details emerged at the inquest. A police constable who had cleaned all the firearms in the store-room three weeks earlier said the revolver that had killed Superintendent Hayward and his son was definitely not loaded. The officer remembered checking it and tying a box of ammunition to the firearm with string. At the inquest the constable said that anyone handling the revolver would have had to untie this string. A cursory inspection revealed that the box of ammunition had been torn open at one corner, and that two rounds were missing.

So what happened on that fateful Saturday? The bullet that killed Frank Hayward had entered his head at an angle from above, and the muzzle of the revolver had been in close proximity to the victim when fired, probably around six inches from the head. These facts seemed to indicate that Frank had been stooping when he was shot, which made the suicide and accidental death theories seem unlikely. The superintendent had told Sergeant Bell that his son had received the fatal wound after picking up the gun, yet the facts indicated that Frank was stooping when he was shot.

There was no doubt about the cause of the superintendent's death. He had shot himself, and this act of suicide was thought to have been triggered by the shock he had experienced at witnessing the death of his own son.

If a murder and a suicide did take place, what was the motive? In all the dialogue of devotion uttered about his son, Superintendent Hayward made virtually no mention of Mrs Hayward, and some thought that this indicated that the superintendent's marriage was a disharmonious one. The policeman's oft-repeated remark about life being unbearable without his son does not say much for his relationship with his wife. But even so, why on earth would a devoted father suddenly decide to kill his own son in cold blood?

THE STADIUM STEPS MURDER

During September 1960 Valerie Sellers, an attractive 19-year-old waitress from Gronant, Flintshire, proudly introduced her boyfriend to her parents. Her sweetheart was John Christopher McMenemy, a 23-year-old Liverpudlian with red hair and a rather pallid complexion. The young man asked Valerie's father, Isaac, for permission to marry his daughter and, after much deliberation, Mr Sellers gave his consent. The couple suffered a few ups and downs, however, and their wedding plans were postponed. Then, on 30 July 1961, while McMenemy was staying at Valerie's home, Mr Sellers confronted the young man and asked him if he really had any intentions of marrying his daughter. McMenemy said he had, and Valerie told her father she wanted the wedding to go ahead. But half an hour afterwards McMenemy suddenly told Valerie: 'I never will marry you.'

Mr Sellers assured his heartbroken daughter that McMenemy's decision was for the best as he was unemployed and would therefore be unable to maintain her. Before he went to bed that night, Mr Sellers gave McMenemy half-a-crown (twelve and a half pence) to pay for his bus fare home, and McMenemy left the house.

On 12 August, he returned to the Sellers' home to repay the £3 and ten shillings (£3.50) he owed Valerie's father. Mr Sellers took the money and bluntly told McMenemy he was no longer welcome at the house and advised him to return to his hometown. McMenemy left in a huff.

On his way to bed at around midnight Mr Sellers

looked into his daughter's bedroom and saw her sleeping. But at 5.30am, when he went to wake her for work, Valerie's bed was empty. He suspected the obvious: she had sneaked out of the house in the early hours to rejoin her barred lover. What Mr Sellers did not know at this point was that he would never see his pretty young daughter alive again.

Five days after the moonlight flit Valerie and McMenemy turned up in Warrington, where they managed to hitch a ride up to Glasgow in the car of Edward O'Sullivan. At the end of the journey McMenemy secretly produced a sheath knife and hid it under the car's dashboard without the driver's knowing. After a short stay in Scotland, Mr O'Sullivan took McMenemy and Valerie to Liverpool. As McMenemy left the car, he put his hand under the dashboard and, this time in full view of the driver, retrieved the knife he had secreted there. O'Sullivan was very uneasy about McMenemy's intimidating behaviour, and was only too glad to see the back of the hitch-hikers.

On the following morning, Sunday 20 August, at around 1.40am, two policeman walking down Bixteth Street, towards Tithebarn Street in Liverpool city centre, observed a couple, whom they later learned to be McMenemy and Valerie, with their arms around one another, walking towards the Liverpool Stadium, the city's famous boxing venue, off Old Hall Street. The officers noticed that Valerie seemed to be crying.

At precisely 3.48am John McMenemy entered a telephone call box at the Pier Head and dialled 100.

'Which number do you require?' the operator asked.

McMenemy paused, then told the operator to take a message. He said that there was a body at the top of the steps of the Liverpool Stadium.

'Where are you speaking from?' said the operator.

McMenemy hung up, then strolled to a waterfront refreshment stall where he sat chain-smoking and drinking cup after cup of coffee. The police, meanwhile, were working with the Post Office to trace the night caller, and within a matter of minutes a wireless message was transmitted to Constables Smith and Walton, who were on motor-patrol duty near to the scene of the reported crime.

Shortly before 4am their Land Rover pulled up at the stadium and the two officers ran to the building's main entrance. On the steps they found the heavily bloodstained body of Valerie Sellers lying with a raincoat draped across her. Near to her head was an unusual clue: a man's tie. One of the officers lifted the raincoat and saw that the young woman had obviously died from multiple stab wounds to her chest and stomach. There were 14 wounds in all. Liverpool Stadium, world-renowned temple of the noble art, now resembled a Mayan sacrificial altar.

The police and the Post Office were remarkably swift in narrowing down the source of the telephone call, and a matter of minutes after the discovery of the body, Smith, Walton and another police officer arrived at the Pier Head. McMenemy had been waiting for them, and before the policemen spotted him, he slipped away from the coffee stall and hurled the silver coins and the pound note he had taken from Valerie's purse into the Mersey.

The three policemen approached McMenemy, and one of them instantly noticed that he was not wearing a tie. Constable Smith said that he was making enquiries into the very recent murder of a young woman and asked

McMenemy if he could account for his movements during the past hour.

'I've been walking about,' was all that McMenemy could offer by way of an alibi.

During the questioning an officer noticed the bloodstain on the cuff of McMenemy's right sleeve, as well as a reddish stain on his right hand. As the suspect was being taken to the rear of the coffee stall for further interrogation, McMenemy suddenly said: 'It's in my back. In my waist band.'

From McMenemy's belt one of the officers withdrew a sheath knife, positioned at the base of his back.

McMenemy then said, morosely, 'She was my girlfriend. I stabbed her once and she groaned so I kept on to put her out of her misery.'

Constable Smith cautioned McMenemy and he was taken to the bridewell, where he was again searched and interviewed at length by Detective Inspector Wade. The search yielded three articles which had belonged to the dead girl: a cigarette lighter, a purse and a bracelet engraved with the words 'Chris and Val' ('Chris' referred to the middle name by which McMenemy chose to be known.) During the interview with Inspector Wade, McMenemy made a full confession and revealed how a petty row over money had cost Valerie Sellers her life.

He explained: 'She would not give me the money. So I stabbed her, but when she started gurgling I decided to finish her off. It is my fault. I want everyone to know what happened.'

In chilling detail his statement went on: 'First, I did not mean to kill her, but when she was arguing about the flat I told her I wanted some money and I was going to get some rum and go away. She would not give it to me,

198

and said, "You can have your own, but you are not having mine."

'I said, "I am having it!" and grabbed her purse. She grabbed it back. I had my knife in my hand. I had been cutting a match. I told her if she did not give me the purse I would stick the knife in her. She said she would not give it to me, so I stuck the knife in her stomach and grabbed the purse. She grabbed my hand and was holding the knife. We fell down the stairs, struggling. She was calling my name. I stabbed her a few more times. I pulled my tie off with the other hand and put it round her throat, knowing that she was dead. I laid her down on the floor. That's all there is. I went around buying coffee and cigarettes out of the money in her purse. She had just under £3. First I was going to make a run for it, but I got thinking about her so I went down to the Pier Head and walked around, thinking, and I realised it was hopeless to run.'

Four days after the murder Mr Sellers was taken to the city mortuary to identify the body of his daughter.

Home Office pathologist Doctor Charles Arthur St Hill carried out the post-mortem and recorded the cause of death. Miss Sellers had died from multiple stab wounds. The attack had been so ferocious that four ribs had been severed; one wound to the stomach was five-and-a-half inches deep.

The pathologist also revealed that Valerie had been two months pregnant when she died.

John Christopher McMenemy was tried at Liverpool Crown Court on Wednesday, 1 November 1961. He did not give evidence and no witnesses were called in his defence. His counsel, Mr J S Watson Q.C., referring to the fatal quarrel, said McMenemy 'may have taken some of her property ... but,' he argued, 'these two people were in love. They wanted to marry each other. Persons in love regard each other's property as their own.'

Lord Chief Justice Parker reminded the jury, however, that the capital charge was of 'murdering Miss Sellers in furtherance of theft.'

McMenemy was found guilty and sentenced to death. The date of his execution was set for 22 November, but on 18 November the case was heard by the Court of Criminal Appeal. Mr Watson, again representing McMenemy, asked the court to substitute a verdict of manslaughter on the grounds of diminished responsibility. The appeal was dismissed and 8 December became the new execution date; but on 24 November a reprieve was recommended by the home secretary, and the death sentence was commuted to life imprisonment.

A Fatal Attraction

In 1913 a fine new church called the Temple of Humanity was established at 46 Upper Parliament Street in Liverpool. The religion or, rather, philosophy of those who attended the church was known was Positivism, a belief-system founded by Auguste Comte, the French philosopher and sociologist. The Positivists do not worship God, but are devoted to humanity and strive for the welfare of mankind. The Positivist creed was viewed by many as too abstract, and the adherents of the philosophy were, and still are, few and far between.

Today the Temple of Humanity is still standing, but is now known as the Third Church of Christ, Scientist. This building was the innocent focus of a series of dreadful deeds perpetrated one autumn evening in 1913. The seed of the tragedy was sown some years before when Mr Sydney Style, a prominent solicitor, and a leader of the Positivists, was introduced to strikingly handsome young Everton, William MacDonald. A carpenter and an ardent socialist, 20-year-old MacDonald was highly interested in joining the Positivists sect, as he believed that their creed dovetailed with his Marxist beliefs. So MacDonald attended one of the soirées that were held every Thursday evening at Number 69 Hope Street, the home of Style and his wife.

At these weekly evening parties MacDonald became acquainted with other Positivists and spent many an hour passionately discussing his views on socialism and extolling dialectical materialism. But MacDonald had another passion, and it was one he never dared admit, for she was 42-year-old Miss Mary Crompton, the beautiful daughter of the late shipping magnate Albert Crompton, who had also been the co-founder of the Liverpool Positivists. Mary's grandfather Sir Charles Crompton, had been a renowned and much-respected Justice of the Queen's Bench from 1852 until his death in 1865.

Mary Crompton was a very kind and understanding individual who always found time to help people in need. She was well-educated and fluent in many languages, but the one thing that she seemed to lack in her life was a man, although she was very attractive and desired by many of the red-blooded males in the sect. One infatuated admirer was 24-year-old Paul Gaze, an orphan who had been adopted by Miss Crompton, along with his brother. Paul had been born within a church of the sect, but had lost both his parents while an infant, and Miss Crompton had stood as a sponsor for him and his brother, and devoted much time and money promoting the interests of the two men. Mary showed particular fondness for Paul Gaze, and when he went to work in Africa as the representative of a chemical factory, Mary corresponded regularly with her protege.

Then, in August 1913, Gaze returned from Africa and Mary was surprised at how much the young man had grown and how manly he had become since she last saw him in person. On many occasions during his teens and adulthood, Gaze confronted his patroness with his passion for her, but she always rejected it. The nature of the love she gave was strictly platonic. Gaze had met and married a stunning young Portuguese girl in Africa, and been married there in accordance with the marriage rites of the Temple of Humanity. When he returned home to Liverpool, he went to stay in his lodgings at Number 62 Grove Street, Edge Hill, and his new wife went to stay at

Mary Crompton's house at Number 81 Bedford Street South. By the rules of the Temple of Humanity, it was deemed necessary for a man and wife, after going through the civil ceremony of marriage, to take a vow of chastity for three months, and afterwards, if they found that their tempers were compatible, their marriage was ratified by the Temple officials. The three months of probation were very nearly at an end when an unforeseen tragedy was to strike. During this time, Mary Crompton would sit in the drawing room of her palatial home, talking to Mrs Gaze in her own native tongue of Portuguese, and sometimes in French, the young lady's second language. Mary learned just how much Paul's wife loved him. As soon as their marriage was fully sanctioned by the sect, Mrs Gaze wanted to start a family.

The green-eyed monster of jealousy reared its ugly head in William MacDonald, who saw it all wrongly. MacDonald thought Mary, the object of his secret love, was becoming increasingly fond of Paul Gaze, and he could not allow that. All of his Marxist ideals of common ownership were applicable to the material world, but as far as Miss Crompton's benevolence was concerned – he wished that to be directed to him alone.

So, on the Tuesday night of 7 October 1913, at 9.30, emotionally torn MacDonald armed himself with a revolver and a weighted stick, and went to the house of Richard Price Roberts, the copper engraver who had introduced him to the Temple of Humanity. As far as the demented MacDonald was concerned, Roberts was another rival. He had also been getting a bit too familiar with Miss Crompton of late.

MacDonald reached Roberts's home in the Islington area of Liverpool and waited. He could turn back now or go through with his psychopathic plan. He rang the doorbell. A few moments later the door opened wide and Roberts himself came out. Almost immediately, MacDonald brought the metal-tipped stick down hard on his head, then drew the revolver and fired at him twice. The first shot missed by an inch and the second passed straight through the victim's nose.

MacDonald ran away, leaving his former friend with blood spraying from his face and a badly injured head, though he was still alive.

Ten minutes later, as bad luck would have it, Paul Gaze happened to meet William MacDonald on the street, and he invited the jealous carpenter to his lodgings on Grove Street. At precisely 10.15pm, the maidservant at the lodging house heard two loud bangs which sounded just like a cane being rapped hard on the front door. They were in fact, gunshots, and when the servant went to investigate she found the door of Gaze's apartment open. Inside she found Gaze dead on the hearthrug with a neat red hole in the centre of his forehead and a wound to his chest where the other bullet had penetrated his heart. Paul Gaze was dead. He wore a puzzled look on his face and his eyes stared at the ceiling.

As this shocking murder was being discovered, William MacDonald was hurrying through the chilly autumnal night to Bedford Street South, just a few minutes' walk away from Gaze's lodgings. MacDonald reached Number 81, where his beloved Miss Crompton lived. She had taken the poor carpenter under her wing, taught him music, and taken a deep interest in his welfare, but that had not been enough for MacDonald. He had fallen in love with Mary Crompton, a woman more than twice his age, and she had not even noticed the way he felt about her. A case of so near and yet so far; why couldn't she see that William loved her? We'll never know now.

He hammered on the doorknocker and waited. The maid answered and MacDonald asked to see Miss Crompton. 'Miss Crompton has just retired to her room,' the maid told him, and was about to close the door, but the young man pleaded to see the lady of the house.

'It's a matter of the utmost urgency, and I must see her at once,' he pleaded.

Again the maid said her mistress had just retired but MacDonald was insistent. The servant relented and showed MacDonald into the sitting-room. A few minutes later, Mary Crompton, the innocent victim of her own fatal attractiveness, came downstairs to greet him. She entered the sitting room. William MacDonald came face to face with the object of his unrequited love. He raised the revolver, pointing its barrel at her temple, and fired, killing her instantly. The single shot startled Paul Gaze's young wife from her sleep in the bedroom upstairs, and she awoke with a fright, not yet aware that her husband was dead and that she was now a widow. The maid rushed to the sitting room, but before she could enter, there was a second loud bang, followed by a thud. MacDonald had placed the barrel of the revolver against his own head and pulled the trigger. He died three hours later at the Royal Infirmary in Pembroke Place.

The double murder and suicide cast a ghastly shadow of shame over the Positivists, and they eventually disbanded. In 1947, the statue that had symbolised the sect – a mother and child – was taken down from its arched recess, high on the front wall of the former Temple of Humanity.